FRIENDS OF ACPL

**ALLEN COUNTY PUBLIC LIBRARY
FORT WAYNE, INDIANA 46802**

You may return this book to any agency, branch,
or bookmobile of the Allen County Public Library

all the damned angels

all the damned angels

by
William Muehl

A Pilgrim Press Book
Philadelphia

Allen County Public Library
900 Webster Street
PO Box 2270
Fort Wayne, IN 46801-2270

Copyright © 1972 United Church Press
All rights reserved.

Library of Congress Catalog Card Number 77-185414
ISBN 0-8298-0230-4

to my sons,
Timothy and Jonathan

contents

Prologue   11

I

1. God Has No Pride   15
2. The Cult of the Publican   23
3. To Hell with Acceptance   32
4. The Energies of God   40
5. The God Who Came in out of the Cold   49

II

6. The Good Guys and the Bad Guys   59
7. Artists and the Real World   69
8. The Quitters   77
9. Preach What You Practice   84

III

10. The Uses of Alienation   91
11. The Two Faces of Faith   99
12. The Christian Conspiracy Against Man   107
13. Man in Free Fall   116

Epilogue   125

3 1833 03223 1026

prologue

Many years ago when my wife and I had a son in nursery school we received at his hands one day a message that chilled our blood. It was a mimeographed note which announced a Christmas pageant and urged all parents to avail themselves of this great cultural opportunity. Since Mrs. Muehl and I feel about Christmas pageants the way rats are reputed to feel about sinking ships, we began straightaway, as the Bible has it, to make excuses. When we learned, however, that our four-year-old was to play the part of a shepherd in the manger scene we decided that it was as foolish to make a principle of not attending Christmas pageants as it would be to make a principle of attending them and agreed that if we happened to be in the neighborhood of the school that morning we might drop in.

That morning, after cancelling two classes and nearly running over a policeman, I happened to be in the neighborhood. And when I entered the auditorium I discovered to my not-very-great surprise that my wife was already seated in the front row.

For a time all our worst fears were more than justified. A group of ungainly upper-class pupils paraded their mediocre talents across the stage in a series of performances verging on the obscene. Mrs. Muehl and I commented objectively on these aesthetic atrocities, to the distress of the hopelessly biased parents in our vicinity.

At last the teacher in charge announced that the manger scene would be presented by the Connecting Class. The houselights dimmed, the school janitor sneaked on stage with a box of straw, and a purple spot focused erratically about halfway between the pillars of the proscenium arch.

Then from the wings came *three* virgin Marys, who arranged themselves coyly around the creche and waved to their relatives in the audience. A vague uneasiness came over me. I feared for a moment that we were about to witness the promulgation of a new dogma—group childbirth. But my wife, who is somewhat more sophisticated than I am in such matters, pointed out that the school had, over the course of the years, acquired three costumes for the virgin Mary. So, by the strange logic which seems to govern pageants, there had to be three virgins.

The virgins were closely followed by two Josephs who took up sullen postures near the box of straw and stood there picking their noses.

Next came the angels, about twenty little girls dressed in diaphanous white gowns and sporting immense gauze wings. They deployed themselves with suspicious symmetry across the platform. Then the shepherds appeared, an equal number of small boys dressed in burlap sacks and clutching an assortment of saplings which purported to be crooks.

At this point an unfortunate discovery came to light. In order to be sure that the angels and shepherds would strike a pleasantly balanced array on stage, the drama coach had made a series of chalkmarks on the floor. A circle for each angel and a cross for each shepherd. She had urgently instructed the children that they were all to find and stand on appropriate symbols. But unwisely this marking had been done when the pupils were wearing their ordinary clothes, shorts, skirts, and overalls. When the angels came on in their flowing robes, each of them covered not only her own circle but the adjacent cross as well.

The shepherds, driven by God knows what demonic impulse to indiscreet obedience, began looking for their places. Angels were treated as they have never been treated before. And at last one little boy, who had suffered about all such nonsense that he could handle, turned toward the wings where the teacher in charge was going quietly mad and announced angrily, "These damned angels are fouling up this whole show. They've hidden all the crosses!"

Needless to say his mother and I were greatly embarrassed.

The pageant is over, the embarrassment has passed, and the child is a man. But his furious proclamation still strikes me as a trenchant comment on the human predicament. We are, indeed, "damned angels," possessors of gifts and insights which we turn to works of destruction, victims of burdens and infirmities which become occasions for glory. The rich pageant of life is often fouled up by our rigid moralism and the cross is hidden beneath the flimsy fabric of our simple piety. With the best intentions we do the worst thing, and then perform miracles of love almost by accident. Our flesh drives and afflicts us from birth to death. But we have the gall to affirm that it once sheltered the Eternal.

There are men wise and good enough to walk with God and see visions of heaven. I have had to be content with damned angels and the facts of life. It is of these that I have written in the pages to come.

I

1

god has
no pride

Early in the last century, in the days when the great fleets of sailing ships went out of New Bedford to scour the oceans of the world for whale oil, the most famous skipper of them all was Eleazar Hull. Captain Hull took his vessel into more remote seas, brought home greater quantities of oil, and lost fewer crewmen in the process than any other master of his time. And all this was the more remarkable, because he had no formal navigational training of any kind. When asked how he guided his ship infallibly over the desert of waters, he would reply, "Well, I go up on deck, listen to the wind in the riggin', get the drift of the sea, and take a long look at the stars. Then I set my course."

One day, however, the march of time caught up with this ancient mariner. The insurance company whose agents covered the vessels of Captain Hull's employers declared that they would no longer write a policy for any ship whose master did not meet certain formal standards of education in the science of navigation. Captain Hull's superiors could understand this new rule. But they were at a loss to know how to approach the proud man whose life had been spent on the bridge and tell him that he must either go back to school or retire. After some consultation they decided to meet the problem head on. Three of the company's top executives waited on Captain Hull and put their dilemma as tactfully as possible.

To their amazement the old fellow responded enthusiastically. He had, it appeared, always wanted to know something about "science," and he was entirely willing to spend several months studying it. So the arrangements were made. Eleazar Hull went to school, studied hard, and graduated near the top of his class. Then he returned to his ship, set out to sea, and was gone for two years.

When the skipper's friends heard that he was putting into port again, they met him in an informal delegation at the docks. They inquired eagerly how it felt to navigate by the book, after so many years of doing it the other way.

"It was wonderful," Captain Hull responded. "Whenever I wanted to know my position, I'd go to my cabin, get out all the charts, work through the proper equations, and set a course with mathematical precision. Then I'd go up on deck, get the drift of the sea, listen to the wind in the riggin', and take a long look at the stars. And correct my computations for error."

This is very much the way of man with God, isn't it? Most of us these days take our rationality with considerable seriousness. We feel an obligation to work out an approach to life which has, if not intellectual precision, at least an element of consistency about it. We may not study the philosophers. But we have heard of them. And we live always in the shadow of the "laboratory," that symbol of scientific rigor which reminds us that one man's opinion is *not* as good as every other's. We often worry so much about the reasonableness of our behavior that we lose the will to act. And we frequently exhaust the patience of family, friends, and even those with whom we are only slightly acquainted presenting careful rationalizations for what we think and do. In an important sense we are children of the enlightenment, heirs of the age of reason.

But on the other hand, when we are called upon in particular situations to make decisions, we ordinarily do so on the basis of a weird mixture of memory, emotion, conditioned response, and fragments of wisdom. We live forever in tension between the ideal image of the proper moral posture and an embarrassed scramble to avoid hating ourselves the next morning. We are the victims, on the one hand, of a deeply felt need to reason; and, on the other hand, of myriad subtle, subrational pressures never fully identified.

It is the beginning of wisdom in religion, and a thing which too few of us understand, that it is primarily the realm in which one deals honestly with himself. The basis of an enduring faith in the reality of God is confidence in the eternal meaning of his own personal history.

Now the moment one says something of this kind, many of his listeners begin to moralize the real meaning out of the statement. That is, they make of it an exhortation to admit their *moral* infirmities, to confess their unclean thoughts, inordinate desires, and multitudinous malfeasances. I sometimes think that the greatest problem of piety in America is that ardent puritanism which cannot distinguish between honesty and shame and therefore supposes that it is being most candid when it is merely embarrassed.

The really difficult honesty which makes up in my mind the chief ingredient of religion cuts more deeply than stammering confessions about what happened when the lights went out. It is the humiliating recognition that man is not an intellect which administers the splendid potencies and chaotic impulses of a subordinate flesh, but an interaction of mind and sense so intricately wrought in the depths of the earth that no finite being can ever distinguish one from the other. And the recognition that this tortured, often self-degrading complexity is the creature and instrument of a God who is utterly without pride, a God who is willing to exploit any emotion, lay hold upon every fear, bait traps with pleasure, and harness all energies to his own ulterior purposes, a God who is willing to stoop as low as necessary to get through the arches of the mind and into the human heart.

I remember as a boy feeling keenly the obligation to make an intellectual decision about the existence of God. It was all very well to go to Sunday school to keep your parents happy, or to be more precise, because they made you go. And even joining church was not too great a price to pay for the use of the gym and membership in the youth group. But I felt quite sure that at some point a man owed it to himself to sit down, assemble all the evidence, and settle the ontological question once and for all.

Well, one thing and another delayed this weighty business until a day dawned in which I began to realize that I was really motivated in the proposed venture by a sense of obligation to God to make a rational and, therefore, intellectually respectable decision about him. To gather the data, sift it carefully, examine the findings, and say to the One who moved through every fiber of my being, "Relax. You may exist."

This discovery was prompted in part by a box of soda crackers that often stood on the kitchen table at which I ate my lunches as a child. On the box of crackers there was a picture of a sailor boy holding a box of the same crackers on which there was a picture of a sailor boy holding a box of the same crackers on which there was a picture of a sailor boy holding a box of the same crackers on which . . . Well, you see what I mean. I have since learned to dismiss that problem, as one dismisses so many other problems, with a phrase. In this case "infinite regression." But before someone gave me the magic words I spent a lot of time worrying about those sailor boys and cracker boxes. Where did they end? Or did they end? Was I sitting hunched over a bowl of soup peering into eternity, an eternity in which sailor boys and cracker boxes went on and on, world *without* end?

In a sense I was peering into eternity. Because I was learning something about the nature of God. One can never get behind his presence in history in order to make objective judgments about his existence. Archimedes said that he could lift the world, if he had a place to rest his lever. Where do you rest your lever in order to lift God off your back? "If I take the wings of the morning," said the psalmist, "and dwell in the uttermost parts of the sea, even there thy hand shall lead me, and thy right hand shall hold me (Ps. 139:9-10)." "You did not choose me," said the Lord. "I chose you (John 15:16)."

It is not a thrilling thing to discover that one has fallen into the hands of God. Some would-be autonomy in a man is outraged by the experience and struggles to retrieve a measure of its dignity. So we often cast about for an indication of the mode or moment in which the sovereignty of the Eternal raised its proprietary standard in our lives. Perhaps there was some mysterious writing on a wall? A strangely combustible bush? An abnormally articulate dove? (Would you believe an attack of heartburn during Sunday school?)

But even these undergarments of self-respect are soon in tatters. It may be that you have two left feet, so that you tend to spend more time on "serious matters" than those of your friends who can dance. Perhaps you get sleepy earlier in the evening than most people, and there came to be applied to your life the dull edge of the old adage "Early to bed, early to rise; and you'll never meet any regular guys." Possibly your grandmother gave you books about God and the moral life; and one weekend you forgot to go to the library before it closed and were stuck on a rainy Sunday afternoon with nothing to read but the meditations of Billy Sunday. Oh, what a distressing thing it is to discover that the God of Abraham, Isaac, and Jacob, the Creator of heaven and earth, can be found even in the meditations of Billy Sunday!

"I fled Him down the nights and down the days; I fled Him down the arches of the years; I fled Him down the labyrinthian ways of my own mind; and in the mist of tears I hid from Him and under running laughter." * This is the experience voiced so powerfully by Francis Thompson in *The Hound of Heaven.* But with the poet's license Francis made it all sound a bit too dramatic. The

---

* Francis Thompson, *The Hound of Heaven* (New York: Dodd, Mead & Co., 1922). Used by permission.

approach of God is less like the baying pursuit of a hound than the invasion of mice into a pantry or ants into a picnic basket. "The day of the Lord will come like a thief in the night (1 Thess. 5:2)." It certainly will. One morning you wake up and find it there. The critical moment for casting balances and making decisions has slipped by silently in the darkness. And now it is impossible to reject God without rejecting all that is best in yourself and the world around you.

But like the checker player who will not concede the game as long as he can move one king back and forth between adjoining squares, our own regal pride never surrenders. And so we look for some way to put our relationship with God upon a sound contractual basis, some way to incorporate the human personality, some way to protect ourselves against claims which run beyond the amount of our voluntary investment in the human enterprise, some kind of fictitious entity with which God must deal, so that he cannot break through the corporate structure and get his hands on our hidden personal assets.

It is, more often than not, this fictitious entity which we send forth to engage on our behalf in the various dialogues of faith, raising impressive problems, asking vexatious questions, and quoting with calm assurance the best scholars and columnists. And always the strategy is the same, to get God to the bargaining table. To get the Eternal to reduce his outrageous claims to quite concrete and reasonable terms.

This is an ancient technique. To try to objectify the problem of faith in some detailed ethical code and make of the code's interpreter a surrogate for God, so that your fictitious self and God's fictitious self can work out something suitable for both: "Tell me, preacher, how close to lying can I come and still tell the truth? This is no metaphysician's question, understand. Out there in the shop where we must live with this contract, it can mean quite practical things. Give me a good enough grievance procedure and I can have all the money and no ulcers. Or how far must I look beyond the end of my own nose? No witty homilies upon the length of my proboscis, please. Just practical advice. How far through the silent night can one shrill cry of pain be heard? How soft must a bed be to cradle me in restful slumber, while all around a world comes tumbling down? How much of my own piece of bread, and my last piece at that, must I give to the hungry child who hates my guts? Be lawyer to my conscience, priest, and get this monkey God off my back."

But how can I be lawyer to your conscience when I am not even master of my own? And upon what paper shall we write a contract that will stand up in the flames of our inner hells? Our common problem, yours and mine, is not that we do not know what we should do in any situation that confronts us, but that we know all too well what we should do. And it is "rather that which we do fear to do than wish't should be undone." We are not so much bewildered in the face of challenge as we are embarrassed by the ease with which the rights and wrongs of any issue fall into place before our eyes; before our minds have analyzed the play and given the commands. It is not the absence of commitment which vexes our hearts, but the urgency of commitments for which we can offer no adequate apology to our brains. We are distressed not because our faith is weak, but because our faith is strong, strong enough to lead us toward destinations which we have not chosen and from which there may be no safe return. And so we make of religion not the stimulus to action but a check upon it, not a direction for our zeal but the boundary beyond which our zeal need not go.

This, I think, is what the greatest of the leaders of the Reformation understood so well. The church in the Middle Ages had become a kind of spiritual corporation, a community of limited liability, a fictitious entity which stood between men and God promising the world to both parties.

But God, like so many other hard bargainers, does not deal with agents. He insists upon confronting the party of the first part. And although this means undignified, even vulgar things, such as waiting in doorways, bribing hotel clerks, peering through keyholes, bugging offices, and wearing false whiskers, this is what God always manages to do. Somehow, somewhere, sometime, when you least expect it, someone will step up to you and say, "Smile. You're on *the* Candid Camera!" And you have had it. The veil is stripped away and you see yourself as you really are. History's open end, the world's eternal dimension.

Capt. Eleazar Hull had more of the biblical about him than his first name. He understood that nothing in the way of conceptual data is as real as man's personal experiences with the elemental forces in which his life was created and by which it will eventually be destroyed. He probably realized that the work done in his cabin with charts, equations, and mathematical precision became a part of his instinctive response to the drift of the sea and the sound of the wind in the rigging. But Captain Hull remembered the most important thing, that the one who must make the final decision and live or die by what he decides is the whole being. This, then, is the one who must set the course. And he is a fool who tries to delegate that task to any one fragment of his person. If there is a God, he penetrates every aspect of creation. And there is no place available from which to examine him with an objective eye. If there is no God, neither piety nor wit can call him into existence. And the only thing more futile than the effort to fabricate the divine from bits and pieces amputated from man is an attempt to discover the Eternal in some small corner of the human mind.

2
the cult of the publican

There are people in this world who do not wear well. Men and women who impress us favorably upon first meeting, but prove disappointing upon repeated contact and closer scrutiny.

Sometimes our disenchantment results from the discovery of character traits which did not appear in the original encounter. We conclude that so-and-so appeared to be a charming fellow and undoubtedly has many splendid qualities, but . . . At other times our change of mind arises not from the appearance of new data so much as from the too frequent appearance of the same old data. A different perspective upon qualities which had once seemed appealing. The chap who was terribly funny with a lampshade on his head or impressively profound with his quotations from Camus and Sartre upon the occasion of our first contact is often less amusing under the third and fourth lampshade and something short of profound as we hear the same lines from the same authors repeated for the tenth time. Some people do not wear well.

For me this has long been true of the publican who upstages the Pharisee and makes himself the star of the eighteenth chapter of the book of Luke. His psychological welcome wears thin with amazing speed. Oh, there is something impressive about him at first reading. We see him enter the temple bowed down under a sense of his own unworthiness. He fears to approach the altar and stands at a distance, not even daring to lift his eyes to heaven. He asks nothing of God, but forgiveness for his sinful life. Viewed for the first time, especially in contrast to the self-righteous Pharisee in a single vignette, he makes a winsome picture. And on the basis of this original good impression he is able to score his point in repeated readings of the familiar story.

But if we are able to react honestly to the Bible and admit such reactions to ourselves; we must confess, I think, that after a while, perhaps after the fortieth or fiftieth recitation of the incident, our feelings for the publican undergo a change.

Nathaniel Hawthorne in his novel *The Marble Faun* has one of his characters complain about a bit of statuary which catches the human figure in a transitional posture. The living form, he objects, should never be frozen by the artist in such a halfway position that one viewing it for the second or third time longs to cry out, "Well, get on with it. Throw it or drop it. Stand or fall. Live or die. But don't just hang there in between!"

Isn't this something of what we all feel about the *moral* posture of the penitent publican? As we encounter him going through his ritual of self-abnegation for the fifty-first time, we may be forgiven for supposing that this thing has turned into a career, or at least an avocation. Sometimes in my mind's eye I can see him raising his children to follow in his footsteps: "Now, kiddies, when you enter the temple you must on no account approach the altar. Stand at a humble distance, and for pity's sake, don't raise your eyes. Bring your arm up in a full swing and strike the breast just below the collarbone. Now all together. Let's take it once more from the top. And this time make your daddy proud of you."

Well, you will perceive, I trust, that I am trying in a fanciful way to approach the problem of divine grace and human responsibility. I mean to suggest that the publican's terrified humility has salutary power *only so long as he does not know that he is being observed and approved.* Only so long as his abject confession is a spontaneous reaction to the presence of God. The moment this fellow reads the book of Luke or even a good review of it and begins to realize that there is saving power in his sense of personal depravity, the well of his naive piety will have been poisoned. Then his allegations of unworthiness become not an honest response to the holiness of the Almighty but mere liturgical exercises, more obnoxious than the self-congratulations of the Pharisee. For if there is anything worse than pride in one's righteousness, it must be pride in one's corruption.

Now admittedly there is great moral power and splendid redeeming force in moments of genuine self-discovery, in the kind of personal recognition in which we catch the publican upon first meeting. But by their very nature such moments are rare and brief. They are like the quick, unexpected glimpses of ourselves that we get from misplaced mirrors or slanted store windows on a commercial street. Glimpses which take us off guard, before we have had time to compose our features and adjust our attire. When without any warning we see briefly what the rest of the world views more often. The anxious squint. The vacuous stare. The glazed indifference or petulant anger. Just a fleeting moment of truth before self-consciousness takes over to remind us who and where we are.

When one is given the opportunity to see himself with this sudden clarity, we might say that he is standing on the border between judgment and mercy. In such a moment he is the naive publican, artless and open. Humility wells up without guile and mingles with the compassion of God in what is surely the essence of grace.

But in that very moment, the publican inevitably loses his innocence. He becomes the sophisticated sinner, reveling in divine love and tempted to make a ritual of self-discovery. Like the disciple Peter in the presence of the transfiguration of Christ, he longs to build a tabernacle and dwell in the midst of this splendid experience.

This is a powerful temptation for all men, is it not? The longing to preserve the first dawn of redemption, the yearning to make the sense of guilt the single active ingredient of piety, the will to define a kind of stylized despair as the most robust spiritual health. It is what Paul Tillich once called man's "last and most intellectual defense against God," the offering not of his whole self but of his sense of unworthiness. Or in the words of Karl Barth, we offer "our little bit of despair" as the currency with which to bargain for salvation.

The tendency is hard to resist and reflects itself in many ways in the life of modern man. The late George Jean Nathan once wrote that he was getting tired of plays in which the leading character was a philosophical bartender, a bank robber who loved canaries, or a prostitute with a heart of gold. (This last he named the "Cosmic Tart.") We are, I think, familiar with the dramatic phenomena of which Nathan spoke. Here is a drama in which the "hero" makes his living selling "rotgut"; but every time he serves a shot he adds a chaser of homely counsel. Or another in which the star is a man who cracks safes. But who, when he learns that his rooming house is on fire, rushes into the flames to save his canary. Or the proverbial woman of the streets. She sells herself over and over again in rituals of commercial love. However, over her bed she keeps a picture of Albert Schweitzer and reads the poems of Santayana in her spare time.

These, you see, are people who *have* read the book of Luke. They have made themselves heirs by adoption not of Christ but of the penitent publican. Their hope of salvation lies not in the transformation of life but in isolated, insulated acts of virtue, by which they are not rescued from their depravity but only made more acutely aware of how total that depravity has become. They have chosen to dwell perpetually on the border between judgment and mercy, offering up their "little bit of despair" as a kind of spiritual bribe.

Nathan misdirected his indignation, however, when he blamed the playwrights who created such characters. The fault lies not with the dramatist, who merely holds the mirror up to nature, but with the moral temper of our whole age. A temper to which an important strain in Christian theology has contributed generously. If the Cosmic Tart has become Broadway's symbol of human hope, it is in large part because the penitent publican has become religion's symbol of God's demand.

One who needs more evidence to support this charge than is afforded by the legitimate theater will find it in abundance on the movie screen and television tube. Both of these media of entertainment repeat many times weekly the same liturgies of pious despair which Nathan condemned in the serious drama. In one story after another the same lesson is pounded home. The only dependable source of moral power is the sinner's moment of self-discovery.

In the classical western *High Noon* the beleaguered town marshall is deserted in his time of trial by everyone, except the local drunk who sobers up and offers his assistance. In *The Magnificent Seven* a Mexican town is saved from bandits by a group of vicious killers whose hearts are mysteriously touched by the people's plight. *The Music Man* tells the tale of River City, Iowa, suffocating in self-righteousness, until redeemed by a confidence trickster who falls in love with one of the fairest of its daughters. And when *Lawman's* Dan Troop sets out to recruit jurors in the trial of a notorious outlaw; only one citizen has the courage to volunteer, Miss Lily, proprietress of the town dance hall, saloon, and God-knows-and-we-can-guess-what-else.

Thus, does the popular culture confirm the darkest suspicions of the serious commentator. Life's vitalities are seen to be the energies generated by sin. Virtue is almost by definition static. It may be the legalistic moralism of the Pharisee or the muscle-bound irrelevance of a Hollywood preacher. But whatever its form, virtue is without strength, zeal, or hope. Where moral force appears in history it is almost invariably depicted as the momentum left over when the sinner, recognizing his guilt, dedicates what is left of his glands to the service of the community. For a brief period he possesses both the energies of sin and the posture of prayer. We must use him quickly, as does the dramatist, before his energies run down and his posture congeals into hypocrisy.

If one accepts this view of things, Augustine's prayer, "Lord, make me chaste, but not yet," may have been more honorably motivated than we have been led to believe.

I suppose that I resent the penitent publican because he is, with that "still unravished bride of quietness," another "foster child of silence and slow time." He is made able to stand forever on the border between judgment and mercy without ever going forward or sliding back. No one can break in upon his moment of self-discovery to ask what he intends to do about what he has so lately learned. None can intrude upon his privacy to speak of implications and consistency. The maiden on the Grecian urn may be frigid, sterile, or a nymphomaniac with a sound sense of strategy. But no one will ever put her to the test. We are only left to wonder whether she will skip so lightly in the eighth month of a difficult pregnancy.

So the philosophical bartender can allow himself the luxury of giving sermons to his clientele, because the play ends before he must choose between preaching and paying the rent. But I had a grandfather who ran a saloon. He was saved by Billy Sunday five times, and until the day of his death he loved to speak of those conversion experiences. His eyes would light up as he talked of the sense of sin, the awareness of his separation from God, the broken spirit, and the contrite heart. Sometimes he even wept a little as he told me of the joy of knowing that no matter how low the sinner, Jesus was always waiting to receive him into grace. Then with an almost ritualistic gesture he would rise from his chair, brush one arthritic palm against another, and say with a wry grin, "But every Monday morning there was that damned saloon."

You see, no one ever rang down the curtain at the right moment for my grandfather. No one ever said, "Here endeth the lesson," and closed the book. He was not permitted to stand forever at the juncture of self-awareness and divine compassion, possessor in perpetuity of sin's vitalities and faith's assurances. There was always Monday morning and that "damned saloon."

Billy Sunday himself seemed to recognize the problem with an almost cynical clarity. He is reported to have said once that the best thing that could happen to any man would be to accept Jesus Christ as his personal Savior, walk out of the tent, be hit by a truck, and killed instantly. Well, that would be grand, wouldn't it? To be taken at the peak of freshness, like the tomatoes in the television commercial, and popped into the bottle in the first flush of grace; kept forever fair.

Men linger on the border between judgment and mercy, I suspect, hoping that something will happen to end the drama before they have to move forward or slide back. We cultivate the fine edge of guilt much as an alcoholic cultivates the fine edge of intoxication. And for the same reason. So our literature abounds in images of despair. Our dramatists celebrate the villain whose only redeeming feature is his consciousness of corruption. With pardonable pride we tell ourselves that no age has faced its depravity more candidly than our own. The penitent publican has become our patron saint; and in his ritual self-abasement, we profess to see the outlines of the truest piety.

Well, it is an easy thing to condemn this religious charade. However, to indict it honestly, is to indict a major aspect of Christian faith itself. The penitent publican does not stand alone in the New Testament. He is one of a large company, those who are glimpsed only briefly and in the moment of self-discovery. These are the people in whom the normal continuities of faith have been ruthlessly abrogated; so that they might witness to one thing, the breadth and abundance of divine grace. The prodigal son, the woman taken in adultery, the one at the well in Samaria, Zacchaeus, the repenting thief on the cross, and a host of others. They appear before Christ, confess their sins, receive salvation, and disappear into the wings until the table of scripture readings or a preacher's whim brings them forth to go through the same ritual another Sunday.

It is the message of Christian faith that Jesus Christ came into the world to save sinners. We believe that God was in him reconciling the world unto himself. But precisely because of this conviction we often seem to limit the Almighty to this single manifestation of his love. We sometimes speak as though God is *only* in Christ and doing nothing but *reconciling*. In a significant sense we have made the Mighty One of Israel the prisoner of the incarnation. From Catholic high mass to Baptist revival meeting the great moments of the faith are those of penitence and forgiveness. And in its most radical form this suggests in the language of Billy Sunday that nothing in the life of faith can ever come up to its beginning. Once you have risen from the dead, what can you do for an encore?

Men linger on the border between judgment and mercy, because that is where the action is. If the primary spiritual force of Christian faith is generated in the conjunction of penitence and compassion, man can never again be as close to God, as plugged in, as it were, to divine power as in the moment of conversion. And so there are people who linger on the border between judgment and mercy, even though it puts them at the edge of the abyss. Because the edge of the abyss is where they have been taught to expect to see God most clearly.

Our age is, I am sure, growing tired of the gospel of guilt. It has confessed its shame and admitted its corruption. And now it challenges Christian theology to speak of what lies beyond repentance. It is asking urgent questions about the content of salvation, the style of the Christian life. The noble prostitute has learned that she cannot be saved in her spare time and begins to mourn her lost virtue. And this is as it should be. For Jesus did not tell the parable of the publican and the Pharisee to publicans in order to show them the inherent value of their guilt. He told it to Pharisees to warn them of the danger of pride. The story was intended to chasten the proud, not exalt penitent depravity.

The distortion of the parable which has given birth to the cult of the publican must be attributed in part, of course, to the sinfulness of man. But this catchall is not the full explanation. A part of the blame, and a large part at that, attaches to the Christian theologian himself and his own best intentions. In our eagerness to make God simple and religion easy to understand we have tried to say all that must be said of ultimate things in the redemptive assurances of the New Testament. We have lifted the truth made manifest in Jesus Christ out of the context of the whole Bible. And it has become in consequence a half-truth, with all the power of the half-truth to condemn what it is meant to serve.

When the word of God's undemanding forgiveness stands apart

from the proclamation of God's full nature, that word can undermine man's sense of the meaning and value of his own life. It drains history of its purpose and turns the tumult of our days into "sound and fury, signifying nothing." If the Christian gospel is to be more than a counsel of pious despair, it must be preached and understood in the context of a creative and demanding doctrine of God's purpose for the world.

I hope that some day the penitent publican will read a *good* review of the book of Luke and discover for all our sakes that he must either move toward the altar in commitment or go down to his house not justified, but condemned.

3
to hell with acceptance

In the music drama *West Side Story* there occurs a marvelous song "Gee, Officer Krupke." It is sung by one of the two street gangs whose warfare makes up the background of the plot, and it speaks with a kind of exuberant directness to the condition of much modern Christian piety.

The boys who do the singing have in the course of their relatively short lives been subjected to almost every imaginable kind of analysis. Sociologists have announced that they are the victims of a disintegrating community. Economists have attributed their behavior to chronic unemployment. Psychologists dismiss their criminal tendencies as the by-products of early insecurity, and so on and on along the spectrum of various determinisms. Experts of every kind have assured the world that the boys are not really *responsible* for their anti-social way of life. And the boys have become quite sophisticated about the whole business.

The song "Gee, Officer Krupke" is sung to characterize the cynical policeman, the cop on the beat whose natural tendency to treat the gang members brutally is constantly being frustrated by well-meaning social workers. In it the boys make fun of their benefactors, mimicking those who have tried so hard to rationalize their misconduct. And one of the closing verses goes as follows:

> O, Officer Krupke, you've done it again.
> This boy don't need a job, he needs a year in the pen.
> It ain't just a question of misunderstood;
> Deep down inside him, he's no good!

Then the whole group swings joyously into the chorus:

> We're no good, we're no good, we're no earthly good.
> The best of us is no damn good.*

Now one could interpret this vignette as simply gallows humor, as nothing more significant than the natural desire of society's victims to hit back where it hurts, where some social tenderness has been exposed. But there is, I think, much more to it than that.

These boys believe that they exist, really exist, as responsible human beings capable of making authentic choices and morally valid decisions. They will not permit themselves to be explained away as social mistakes. They shrewdly perceive that any inter-

---

* Copyright 1957, 1959 by Leonard Bernstein and Stephen Sondheim. Used by permission of G. Schirmer, Inc.

pretation of their behavior, however humane its intention, which assumes that they are not in control of their own destiny destroys their dignity as persons. They are not willing to be loved at the expense of their humanity and would rather be hated as evil people than forgiven into limbo. And so they exult in their corruption. Because in the context of deterministic apologies, it affirms both identity and freedom.

There is, I am sure, something of this same defiant spirit in all of us, especially in our attitude toward God. We resent any form of divine love which threatens the particularities of history and reject any definition of mercy which denies the ultimate significance of our acts.

John Buchan, the distinguished commentator on Scottish life, once noted that in the years following the wars for the covenant there was a dramatic revival of devil worship in Scotland. Pagan altars which predated the Roman Empire were rebuilt upon their original sites and obscene rituals practiced in the dark of the moon.

Buchan attributed this phenomenon to the radically grace-oriented doctrine which had been imposed upon Scottish Christianity by the state church. When you tell men, he said, that their ultimate destiny depends upon some whim of God and is wholly unrelated to the quality of their individual lives, you render their most cherished achievements insignificant and undermine the meaning of existence itself. Men whom God appears to deny even a degree of spiritual autonomy will bargain with Satan to attain it. Those who have been persuaded that they can do nothing to pull down a little heaven are very likely to raise a lot of hell!

From a somewhat different perspective Nikolai Berdyaev called attention to the same problem when he charged that Christian emphasis upon divine mercy, especially Protestant emphasis upon wholly unmerited grace, is one of the major causes of the "demonic materialism" of Western culture. If it is not possible by one's deeds to lay up treasure in heaven, Berdyaev suggested, men are very likely to do the next best thing and lay up treasure on earth.

There *is* something in all of us which needs to find qualitative distinctions in the struggles of daily life, something which hungers to believe that one deed is better than another in ultimate terms. If such distinctions cannot be discovered within the doctrines of Christian faith, they will eventually be inferred from some secular substitute. When a man's work is not given importance by his religion, that work will, as Berdyaev points out, eventually replace his religion as a reason for being.

It is quite a leap from Bernstein to Buchan to Berdyaev. But each of these men saw in his own way the same fundamental truth, that any definition of redemption which denies an ultimate significance to human initiatives in the drama of salvation is self-defeating. Indeed, it is interesting to note that all three went a step further to suggest that such a doctrine may actually condemn those whom it purports to save. Bernstein's street gang rejoiced in its power to be "no damned good." Buchan's Scots made pacts with the devil. And for Berdyaev there was something "demonic" about the materialism of the Protestant West. In short, there are ways of speaking about the mercy of God which are not merely inadequate or confusing but positively destructive to the health of the listener, because they strike at the essence of his humanity.

I suggest that this is true of much of our current preoccupation with the word "acceptance" and its prominent place in the vocabulary of faith. To tell men, as the church does so often these days, that they are "accepted by God," may be no good news at all, but the worst kind of bad news.

The problem begins in the failure of many theologians to take account of some of the most elementary facts of life, psychologically speaking. In their revulsion against natural theology, a number of the church's most distinguished minds seem to have gone at least one step too far and thus lost touch with nature. This can be observed in the assumption popular among clergymen that one persuades men that they are forgiven by proclaiming God's undemanding love over and over again and making the assurance of mercy the central theme of all preaching.

The temptation to do this is, of course, understandable. But if one steps outside the ethos of piety for a moment and brings to bear upon this problem the insights available in other areas of experience, it should become quite clear that nothing makes forgiveness *less* persuasive than much speaking about it. Or, for that matter, much emphasis upon it in any form.

If, for example, a man is unfaithful to his wife and the fabric of their relationship is torn, how does the man know when he has been truly forgiven? Well, it is surely not while his wife continues to tell him that he is forgiven. So long as the little woman sends him off to work each morning bearing the burden of her charity and meets him at the door every night with words of reconciliation, he knows very well that the restoration of their union is not complete. And even when the verbal expressions of forgiveness cease, the penitent adulterer realizes that the fabric of conjugal affection has not been restored so long as the liturgies of special attention continue. His favorite food at dinner, the pipe and slippers laid ready by the easy chair, the television set tuned always to *his* special programs—these are indictments more damning than anything that Perry Mason has to face.

No man is truly forgiven by wife, by children, or by offended friends until he is treated as forgiven, until he is once again subjected to the exploitations and burdens of normal human relationships, as well as to their privileges. The moment in which his wife tosses him the dish towel and says, "All right, Buster, it's your turn to dry," that is when the penitent husband knows that he is once again a member and victim in good standing with the human family.

I have always felt that the parable of the prodigal son ends a bit too soon to be fully persuasive. What happened the morning after the feast of the fatted calf, when the rest of the household pulled itself together and rose to go about the grubby details of the day's work? Did the father once again fall upon his son's neck, kiss him, and repeat the liturgies of reconciliation? Or did he hand the boy a hoe and send him into the fields to be what the young man had offered to be, just one more of the hired hands?

This, you see, is the character of real forgiveness, the assumption that a whole relationship has been reestablished, the assumption that the one forgiven can be taken at his word, held to his promises, and punished for his failures. One may have to forgive seventy times seven, because the assumption of genuine repentance so often proves to be unfounded. But no forgiveness is real which does not take that risk. The function of redemptive love, both God's and man's, is not to make the sinner feel better about his past. It is to give him back his future.

But here we encounter again the self-defeating character of much that is proclaimed as the gospel. For, how can one who sees God's compassion as acceptance, as the suspension of judgment, and the refusal to condemn move out of the liturgies of redemption and into the persuasive reality of expectation? Once more the psychological infirmity of Christian doctrine reveals itself clearly. By dwelling as dramatically as it does upon the symbols and assurances of pardon, theology neglects that without which it becomes mere legalism, words with no convincing ring. In our zeal to deliver the invitation, we forget to enclose directions on how to get to the party. And this absentmindedness makes the sincerity of the invitation suspect. (Like those occasional engraved anachronisms which bid us attend the wedding of an acquaintance which took place yesterday in Hong Kong.)

So it is with the gospel. The more we tell men that forgiveness is acceptance; that mercy is a gift wholly unrelated to any merit of their own; the more persuaded they become that there is a hidden price, a price so high that we are unwilling even to quote it for bargaining purposes. Of course they are right. There is a price for that kind of divine compassion. And I do not mean the blood of Christ. I mean the surrender of the dignity and meaning of human existence. Total abdication of man's power to do anything of ultimate value. *That* is the terrible price of a forgiveness which is ever-present, ever-available, undemanding, and wholly unrelated to the quality of one's life.

James Martineau once said that a man who is forgiven too many times too easily may lose the power to sin and sink to the level of mere natural necessity in his acts. I should prefer to say, rather, that mercy has meaning only when there is a price tag attached to it and when the alternative to paying that price is some kind of final destruction, some version of hell. Whatever the merit of this position as theology, I would defend it as excellent psychology.

You see, the gospel of acceptance assumes an excessive, even an obsessive sense of the meaning of history on the part of the believer. A meaning defined almost entirely in terms of a vertical relationship with God, sometimes called the "spiritual" dimension in every moment. Legalism of all kinds—Orthodox Jewish, conservative Catholic, and pietistic Protestant—puts a moral price tag on every human action. But the price is determined by divine whim and quoted in terms of an eternal currency. Thus to the rigor of discipline which all forms of law impose upon their subjects, divine law adds the terror of mystery, because it appears to bear so little relationship to the causalities and consequences, to the horizontal patterns of visible history. Whatever the original utility of moralistic imperatives, they almost inevitably degenerate into ends in themselves, making a virtue of their irrelevance and a holy mystery of their origins. So that men come in time to try to fulfill them not by rational obedience to their intent, but by sacerdotal liturgies.

Now to go among men who tremble in the presence of a complex body of such irrational rules, who walk in fear of breaking some law which can be neither inferred nor understood in terms of the reasonable needs of daily life; to go among men who believe that they are in danger of being ignited by some cosmic pyromaniac because they have transgressed one of his more obscure house rules or interfered with one of his exotic hobbies; to go among such men and tell them that they are accepted, that they need not worry about the exact meaning of this ordinance or that law, *is* to proclaim good news of the most authentic kind. And the response of such men to that word is very likely to be one of joy and gratitude.

But this is hardly our situation, is it? The people to whom the gospel is to speak today are not huddled fearfully in the shadow of ancient altars, trying to work out the exact implications of rigorous commandments. They are, rather, wandering about aimlessly, troubled by the increasing suspicion that no one literally gives a damn about what they do. The problem of our time is not an obsessive sense of the meaning of human existence, but a terrible dread, a deep anxiety that the whole show is indeed an archaic charade. To tell such men in such circumstances that they are *accepted* without reference to the quality of their lives, is to confirm the worst of their darkest fears.

I suggest that one proclaims the good news to modern man by speaking of the wrath of God and the depths of hell. For it is the anger of God which gives meaning to life and the depth of hell which measures the potentialities of man. In one's relations with God, as in his relations with his fellows, forgiveness is hard to believe in until after the first quarrel. It is in our perpetual quarreling with a god who expects something of us that we come to know that we have been redeemed. Significance and salvation may not be the same thing. But in our age they are inseparable. And even God cannot give significance as a gift.

You see, what is accepted by God is not my life or yours, not the individual's infirm and inadequate responses to the challenge of existence. What is accepted is life itself. In Jesus Christ God gave eternal significance to finite existence and agreed that man would no longer be judged by some mysterious vertical relationship to perfection, but by the creative exercise of his stewardship among the sons of men.

One December afternoon many years ago a group of parents stood in the lobby of a nursery school waiting to claim their children after the last pre-Christmas class session. As the youngsters ran from their lockers, each one carried in his hands the "surprise," the brightly wrapped package on which he had been working diligently for weeks. One small boy, trying to run, put on his coat, and wave, all at the same time, slipped and fell. The "surprise" flew out of his grasp, landed on the tile floor, and broke with an obvious ceramic crash.

The child's first reaction was one of stunned silence. But in a moment he set up an inconsolable wail. His father, thinking to comfort him, knelt down and murmured, "Now it doesn't matter, son. It doesn't really matter."

But his mother, much wiser in such affairs, swept the boy into her arms and said, "Oh, but it does matter. It matters a great deal." And she wept with her son.

Jesus of Nazareth told his disciples that any man who calls his brother a fool stands in danger of the fire of hell. It is a terrible thing for a man to stand in danger of the fire of hell. But there is one thing worse. And that is for a man *not* to stand in danger of the fire of hell!

4
the energies of god

In the early days of the Christian church there lived an eloquent monk who traveled from town to town in Italy preaching the gospel to "all sorts and conditions of men." He spoke on many themes, but like all preachers he had a favorite. His was the beauties of the celibate life. This was the subject to which he addressed himself most often and which evoked his greatest rhetorical power.

One day when he had finished a sermon, he was approached by a lusty peasant lad who had been in his congregation and who had listened with obvious interest.

"Brother," said the young man, "I was much moved by your words. But one thing troubles me. If all men felt as you do, what would happen to the human race?"

The monk smiled wryly and replied, "My friend, have no fear on that score. There will always be enough unbridled carnality abroad to populate even so vast a realm as this earth."

Well, in one respect the monk was right. Men can be counted upon to attend to their procreative responsibilities without special exhortations from the pulpit. If the religious community has a particular duty in this area of life, it is more likely to be to urge some restraint in the zeal with which humanity is threatening to overpopulate the globe.

But there *is* another sense, and an important one, in which the monk's reply to the young peasant was wrong. He obviously assumed that the creativities of life did not need to be fitted into the structure of Christian doctrine, that they could be left to morally neutral or even demonic energies. So far as he was concerned something as essential to the purposes of God as the perpetuation of the human race could be consigned to the custody of "unbridled carnalities."

This attitude is not peculiar to monks who are hung up on celibacy. It represents an important strain in Christian thought, one which can be seen at work in every century and applied to a multitude of human responsibilities. Christianity is embarrassed by the creative energies of God and deeply uncertain about the way in which they fit into the pattern of the moral life.

The perplexity is most obvious, of course, in the realm of human sexuality. From its very beginnings Christianity has taken for granted the usefulness of the sex drive, but has allowed very little place for it in the Christian doctrine of man. Celibacy was made the honored badge of a special vocation, physical desire headed the list of those torments with which Satan was supposed to afflict the righteous, and some later Protestant divines equated sex with original sin itself. (These last frequently recommended biblical texts to be meditated upon during the conjugal act in order to minimize its harmful results!)

One can see the same dilemma at work in the treatment given by many Christian ethicists to the problem of material prosperity. An endless torrent of books and pamphlets has issued from the religious press dealing with the morality of an equitable distribution of the earth's abundance. And the virtue of stewardship is a common theme in Christian preaching. But remarkably little has been written and said about the ethics of *productivity,* about the incentives and rewards by which wealth is created in the first place. Here again one encounters the easy assumption that production will be taken care of by neutral or satanic energies, by the *lust* of man for gain, and that the conscience need concern itself only with seeing that everyone gets a fair share of the booty.

There is, in short, a kind of parasitic quality to Christian theology. It depends for its very existence upon vitalities for which it assumes no serious responsibility and against which it levels some of its most indignant assaults. It is, as I said earlier, embarrassed by the creative energies of God.

Yet, if one were to take up the Bible without prejudice and seek the fundamental characteristic of the God which it reveals, he would find it to be *creativity.* The book of Genesis opens with a magnificent burst of energy. God is portrayed in it as the Creator, the one who makes existence possible.

> Let there be light; and there was light. . . . Let there be a firmament in the midst of the waters. . . . Let the earth put forth vegetation, plants yielding seed, and fruit trees bearing fruit in which is their seed, each according to its kind. . . . Let the earth bring forth living creatures, according to their kinds: cattle and creeping things and beasts of the earth according to their kinds. . . . Let us make man in our image, after our likeness; and let them have dominion over the fish of the sea, and over the birds of the air, and over the cattle, and over all the earth. . . .
> —Genesis 1:1-28

The God of the Bible is before all else the Creator.

And if in the same manner one were to take up the Bible and seek the primary quality of man, he would find it to be creativity. Man is the instrument of divine energy. God's first commission to his creatures is neither to be just nor compassionate but to "be fruitful, and multiply, and fill the earth."

This, I suggest, is a major thrust of the Garden of Eden story. Adam and Eve are set down in a realm of uninhibited creativity. Trees bring forth fruit, animals reproduce their own kind, and all the bounty of nature replenishes itself with untended spontaneity. Man has no responsibilities at all. He can come and go, eat and sleep, and love and rejoice at his pleasure. There is in Eden no such thing as law. The one rule is not so much a commandment as an inevitable implication of this unstructured mode of existence. Man must not eat of the fruit of the Tree of the Knowledge of Good and Evil. Well, this makes sense. If one is to dwell in the milieu of irresponsibility, he must perforce avoid making moral judgments. So long as man remains ignorant of the distinction between good and evil, he is nothing more complex than a manifestation of divine energy.

But man, according to the myth, chooses to be a somewhat more sophisticated part of the cosmic process. He eats of the fruit of the Tree of the Knowledge of Good and Evil. And his existence is immediately transformed. He is driven out of Eden and into history. The decision to choose imposes the burden of responsibility. All the splendid energies of being are subjected to the structures, forms, and duties of historical order. And human freedom becomes a highly qualified gift.

So the second thing that the Bible says about God is that he is the Judge and that he has made man the instrument of his judgment. Just as God the Creator sent his creatures forth to multiply and fill the earth, bearers of his creative commission, so God the Judge commands them to seek truth, make laws, administer justice, and punish offenders.

If one were looking for an Old Testament definition of history, he could probably find it stated most dramatically in the conjunction of those two inherently opposed commissions. History in the Bible is the endless tension between creativity and judgment, energy and form. It is the story of man's tragic struggle to fulfill an essentially contradictory destiny. On the one hand he is a mass of urgent desires which drive him to create, to pile stone upon stone, to pour paint over canvass, to scatter notes across the scale, to add dollar to dollar, and to breed children for whom the earth will soon have no room. But on the other hand, this same man is compelled by divine judgment to hold all that he creates up to the image of perfection, find it shabbily inadequate, smash it to fragments, and start building all over again.

The advent of structure in life is presented in the Bible as punishment, the consequence of human disobedience. And the aptness of this image is easy to understand. In the very nature of things, the relationship between creativity and judgment is one of conflict and suffering. The two are never broken to double harness. No man ever manages to apportion his loyalty and divide it fairly between energy and form. Structure and responsibility are always impositions upon creative passion. And the human spirit is the battleground on which they struggle. Every moment of every day of every human life is one more skirmish in the unending campaign. Richard Wagner rattling the chains of classical composition and a young man testing the virtue of his weekend date have at least this in common, they are driven by creative energies which will not be easily confined.

It is not surprising, then, that men seek to resolve this powerful tension by rejecting one of its component parts, by *trying* to commit their loyalties to one cause or the other, and by denying that both creativity and judgment stand upon equal footing as divine commissions. Small wonder that some become bohemians and beatniks, worshipers of uninhibited creativity, artists by whom the rules of normal communication are rudely flouted and unstructured impulse made a first principle. Nor is it difficult to see how others, men of a different temperament, become authoritarians, devotees of order at any cost, minions of totalitarian masters. The instinct for self-preservation is powerful. It constitutes a perpetual temptation to resolve the primordial tension in favor of one of its poles. Life would be so much simpler and less painful, if we could just make either creativity or judgment the single integrating theme of our existence.

In the book of Job, the Old Testament tells us the story of a man who tried to do this, almost without realizing what he was about.

Job was a moral man. He lived by the letter and spirit of the law. He understood God as the Judge. And he accepted the fact that this reality imposes upon human beings the burden of conscience and injects into history the problem of justice. He fasted and prayed, gave freely to the poor, treated friends and enemies with scrupulous fairness, and raised his children in the fear of the Lord.

But Job made the natural mistake. Being a righteous man he came to suppose that all that needs to be said about the Almighty can be said in the language of justice, that obedience to the will of the Most High consists in the reduction of life's chaotic energies to the structure and discipline of the law. Without realizing what he was doing, Job came to worship something less than the whole God. He tried to subordinate the complex will of the Eternal to one of its own aspects.

Then God acted as the Creator. Goaded by Satan, the story tells us, God moved to create a moral good by setting a test to which Job could respond in faith. But in order to do so God was forced to cut through the neat circle of reciprocities in which Job had come to dwell. For even the Almighty cannot create in the truest sense without tipping old balances and violating existing rules. So Job's life was rudely shaken. His wealth was destroyed, his family slain, and his reputation ruined. And Job felt betrayed. The predictable deity from whom he had come to expect understandable behavior had let him down. God had broken the rules of the game. And Job lamented the day in which he was born, the night in which he was conceived:

> Why did I not die at birth, come forth from the womb and expire? . . . Why is light given to [those], . . . who long for death, . . . and dig for it more than for hid treasures? The arrows of the Almighty are in me; . . . the terrors of God are arrayed against me. [O] that it would please God to crush me, that he would let loose his hand and cut me off!
> —Job 3:11, 20-21; 6:4, 9

And throughout much of the rest of the book Job keeps trying to understand what has happened to him in terms of justice. His friends assure him that he must have sinned in some way in order to merit such terrible afflictions. He keeps asking himself what he has done and assures God that nothing in the realm of reciprocity will explain the intensity of his suffering. Job believed, and rightly so, that as judgment the pain visited upon him and his family was wholly undeserved. "My judge breaks me with a tempest," he cries, "and multiplies my wounds without cause."

God's answer to Job's lament is one of the most widely misunderstood portions of the Bible. Even distinguished scholars who should know better have argued that the Almighty simply browbeats Job, threatens the man into silence by a show of divine power. But this is a thesis which cannot stand up long in the face of any sensitive reading of the words attributed to God in the book of Job itself. For what the Lord does is to show Job the error of trying to understand him in terms of judgment alone. He lifts Job poetically out of the realm of justice in which the man has tried to define existence and lets him look for a splendid moment upon God the Creator. Listen to his words:

> Where were you when I laid the foundation of the earth? Tell me, if you have understanding. Who determined its measurements—surely you know! . . . On what were its bases sunk, or who laid its cornerstone, when the morning stars sang together, and all the sons of God shouted for joy? . . . Have you commanded the morning since your days began and caused the dawn to know its place? . . . Has the rain a father, or who has begotten the drops of dew? From whose womb did the ice come forth, and who has given birth to the hoarfrost of heaven? . . . Can you bind the chains of the Pleiades, or loose the cords of Orion?
> —Job 38:4, 6-7, 12, 28-29, 31

"Look upon me as I really am, Job," cries God. "I am not simply justice to be calculated and counted upon, to be bound by rules, forecast by prophet, and dispensed by priest. I am the mighty One who creates all that is, and my creating hand cannot be restrained by any rules of justice, even my own. What you have suffered is not punishment inflicted by my judgment. It is the torment which the clay always endures in the hands of the potter."

Then Job, seeing for the first time the complexity of creation and realizing that God's creativity makes undeniable demands upon God's justice, understands that the structures of stability and order by which men live must always be broken by thrusts of divine initiation. And he cries, "I have uttered what I did not understand, things too wonderful for me, which I did not know (Job 42:3)."

We human beings have a terrible stake in the realm of reciprocities. In so many ways we are dependent for our comfort and even our very lives upon those balances, those repeated, consistent processes which men call justice. The more man learns about himself the more aware he becomes of the multitudinous systems by which his existence is sustained and his world kept in its place. From the very metabolic balance which makes our bodies function properly to those complicated social arrangements which let us dwell together in relative harmony, we are little systems, miniature spheres of justice, small realms of reciprocity. We want desperately to have today be like yesterday and tomorrow akin to them both. We need to be sure that two and two will always add up to four, that what nourishes in one moment will not poison the next, that people can be counted upon to stand in line, follow the rules, and keep the peace. We long to know God as a benevolent Judge, the guarantor of tranquillity.

But nothing, not even our terrible need, can fetter divine creativity. And creativity always flouts old ways of doing things. The musician who would engender new harmonies often distorts the older ones. The businessman who invents a more efficient process or manufacturing technique frequently renders old methods obsolete, destroys his competitors, and turns honored crafts into quaint hobbies. From the first twinges of morning nausea to the last throes of labor, the birth of a child upsets all kinds of physiological, psychological, and aesthetic balances in the life of a woman.

When men forget that God is, first of all, the Creator, when they persist in trying to understand all that happens to them in life as reflections of divine judgment or mercy; the problems of faith are greatly multiplied. Much of what happens in history, much of what we see as affliction in the world cannot be understood except in terms of God's multiple dimensions. Various forms of suffering make no sense at all unless they are seen as the inevitable results of God's ceaseless creativity. The effort to understand God as Judge only made a tragedy of Judaism. The attempt to interpret God as simply mercy can make a comedy of Christianity.

A few years ago a scientist speaking of cancer said that it might be described as "a burst of undisciplined energy, the life force run amuck." A burst of undisciplined energy, the cells of the human body breaking through the rules that govern their development and multiplication and growing in a burst of irresponsible power. There is a terrible symbolism in this image and in the suffering which it necessarily implies. When the first amoeba was exposed to whatever cosmic forces compelled it to become something more complex, it must have questioned the justice of God. When the lungfish found itself forced by drought to forsake its cool streams and crawl in dusty agony on dry ground, when some cataclysm of nature made the first mammal rise from all fours and walk with faltering steps on two feet, the heavens must have rung with the inarticulate cries of primordial piety. At every stage in the growth of this planet, from whirling flame to modern society, change and pain have gone hand in hand. If at any point in cosmic history God had respected the integrity of old structures and balances, man would not even exist today. The whole enterprise would have stopped short, the memorial to a Creator whose nerve had failed.

Somewhere ages hence when man, or whatever man in the providence of God has become, stands on the frontiers of greatness which you and I cannot even begin to imagine, he may look back across the ages at what we call undeserved suffering, at famine, tempest, earthquake, and myriad natural disasters, and see in these afflictions not the punishing fist of the Judge, but the restless fingers of the Creator.

5

the god who came in out of the cold

There are many aspects of biblical religion which trouble the modern mind. One of the most distressing of them is the movement of the Bible between cosmos and province, the way in which particular parts of Near Eastern geography keep intruding upon the otherwise universal quality of its content.

One finds himself reading along in the Old Testament, for example, gripped by some passage of unusual beauty, keenly aware of its relevance for all men in every age, when with little or no warning he hits the slopes of the hill Mizar, impales himself on one of the cedars of Lebanon, or falls into the hands of those improbable people, the Hermonites.

These are inevitably embarrassing experiences. Most of us are catholic in taste and eclectic in theology. We like to drink truth in its pure form, a clear, distilled liquor from which all the gross flavor of history has been removed. We are thrilled to know that the eternal reveals itself to mankind everywhere. But we get a bit queasy at the allegation that Yahweh spoke to Moses at Horeb. We are moved by prophecy which proclaims the recovery of sight by the blind. But almost disgusted at the picture of Jesus of Nazareth dabbing a mixture of dirt and spittle on sightless eyes near the Pool of Siloam. The abstraction inspires. The incarnation disturbs and repels.

It is this yearning after generalized and abstract religion which accounts in large part, I am sure, for the popularity of such books as Kahlil Gibran's *The Prophet.* For here we have the language of things spiritual manipulated poetically in a historical vacuum. Gibran's prophet speaks to mankind without ever having to address himself to particular men and women in specific historical circumstances. He seems always to be preaching to disembodied minds, never to demented bodies. Whatever else may be the condition of this prophet's hearers, we can be pretty sure that they have no ductless glands. Gibran gives us an appealing preacher, one who stands upon no recognizable local terrain, one who appears to have winnowed the grain of truth and left the chaff on the threshing room floor.

I have heard it suggested by disciples of this prophet that the Bible ought to be expurgated. Not to remove all the fornication and violence. But to get rid of that far greater obscenity, the particular history of a not too particular people. Anyone who is honest with himself must admit the superficially attractive character of that proposal. If we could, with a wave of the hand, eliminate the Perizzites, Canaanites, Gergashites, Hivites, and Jebusites, the Bible would be a lot easier to read. And, incidentally, it would simplify things greatly for Joshua!

But expurgating the Bible would hardly solve our problem. For every aspect of the Christian life involves us in the same dilemma. On all sides the lofty structures of our theology are besieged by the specific clamor of particular people, for tangible benefits. When we try to meditate upon a God who is the prime mover or the ground of all being, we are interrupted by some barbarian praying for the success of the sugar beet crop. Just as we formulate a satisfactory concept of immortality based upon the transcendence of ethical goods, along comes a crank proclaiming the resurrection of her nephew. If we work out a definition of the atonement rooted in the redemptive community, we are likely to be assailed by fanatics who want to be washed in the blood of the Lamb.

All occasions seem to conspire against us. Our prayer books have on one page a moving petition for "all sorts and conditions of men." And on the next page a plea for an end to "these intemperate rains." Our clergymen may preach eloquently and in appropriately abstract language about ultimate things, only to lapse at the end of the sermon into childlike requests for various goodies. And the chief spiritual condition of our friends and neighbors seems to be the endless tension between *hoping* and *fearing* that the Eternal is giving them its undivided attention.

The devices by which men try to rationalize these contradictions are numerous. Sometimes we erect elaborate facades of private and personal interpretation. "Give us this day our daily bread" becomes a plea for spiritual not physical nourishment. Or we may go high church and accept the language of the particular as an antique but mysteriously edifying liturgy. But we can never completely escape the geography of the historic faith and the unhappy feeling that revelation occurs not in spite of the particular in history, but in some sense because of it.

Now in some respects this problem appears in all areas of human existence. Men always find it hard to establish complete rapport between the world of ideas and the cunning realities of their everyday lives. There is always a disturbing discrepancy between theory and practice. We are able to conceive magnificently and bring to pass only a shabby imitation of that conception. And there is a perpetual check upon human pride in those familiar words, "Well, back to the old drawing board."

I have said that this is a problem common to all areas of life. But more often than not we are able to come to terms with it. We recognize that what men dream must finally be expressed within the limitations of what men are. We understand that no vision, however fair, can take on form that is unconditioned by the tools and materials with which men must work. We look with incredulity or disdain upon anyone who cannot accept this fact of life.

When I first moved to Connecticut I was given an opportunity to visit an old colonial house not far from New Haven. My wife and I made a tour of the whole place. Every room breathed into the air something of the atmosphere of the time in which the structure had been built. And the house was occupied by the last surviving descendant of the original owner, a frail old woman in her seventies.

As we stood in the main room talking, I noticed an old rifle hanging over the fireplace. I was struck by its beauty and wanted to take it down and examine it more closely. But as I reached out, the old woman quickly caught my arm and said, "Please don't touch it. It's loaded and might go off."

When I raised an inquiring eyebrow, she went on to say, "My great, great, great grandfather loaded that gun and put it there against the day when he might strike a blow for the freedom of the American colonies."

I drew what I still feel was the logical inference from the situation and asked, "But the old gentleman died before the Revolution?"

"No," my hostess responded, "he lived to a ripe old age and died in 1817. But (and here she smiled wryly) he just never seemed able to generate much enthusiasm for General Washington's rebellion."

It is no wonder that this lady is the last of her line. The miracle is that it lasted as long as it did. But in a sense we all have something of her great, great, great grandfather's blood in us, don't we? We can easily imagine what the old man who put that gun there must have felt. He may have spent many a winter evening in front of the fire and many a summer afternoon under an apple tree dreaming of the day when he would strike a blow for freedom. With the passage of time more and more details probably filled in the outlines of the dream, until at last it turned into a full-length, standard version of what was to come and included a touching scene in which a troop of well-drilled militia would march up to the front door and say, "Benjamin, lead us to victory on the field of honor."

There must have been tears in his eyes as Benjamin anticipated such a moment and composed a speech with which to respond to the invitation, one which doubtless drew heavily upon the classics. But then one April day a group of his less affluent neighbors came by and one of them said, "Ben, there's been a hell of a scrap at Concord. Git yer gun and let's go."

This was not what Ben had imagined. He could see no connection between his concept of revolution and a grubby gang of ruffians setting out for a fight somewhere in Massachusetts. He preferred to wait until history fulfilled itself in more appropriate terms.

Well, we can be amused by a would-be revolutionary who expects a rebellion to start with a flourish of trumpets and be fought by literate gentry with Miltonian phrases on their lips. Most of us understand that revolutions do not come to full flower in the dreams of idealists, but need for their roots a rich compost of irrational and bitter discontent. The rebel who will not dig his hands into such soil is doomed to futility.

And so in other respects. Who can sympathize with the man or woman who longs for the joys of marriage and family life but cannot bring himself to accept the physical component of erotic love? We are bewildered by a painter who wants to portray the human body as it would appear if viewed from all directions simultaneously. And we would ridicule a composer who sat before a piano and wept because he had only two hands.

In most areas of life we come to terms with our humanity and learn that what we dream must be expressed within the limitations of what we are. Wise men spend little time regretting the elemental facts of life.

In the realm of religion, however, we often resist this knowledge with all the stubborn pride of the indignant mind. The very man who is most determined to establish his human relationships on the basis of a candid realism is the most tempted to insist that he can deal with God only while standing on holy ground. Obviously there are mixed motives behind such strong efforts at theological disengagement. To some extent men try to hold God at mind's length, because they have serious misgivings about what he might notice in any really intimate contact. (Here we advance the argument of those who once urged that the capital of the United States be moved out of Washington so that foreign visitors and diplomats would not be affronted by the spectacle of human slavery!)

But this is only a part of the truth. And the less important part at that. We act, I am sure, not simply in self-defense, but also in response to a kind of misguided piety, an unwillingness to involve the eternal in our finite ventures.

It is said that the comedian Groucho Marx once turned down an invitation to join an exclusive club with the words, "I wouldn't belong to a club that would take in a guy like me." This is the attitude behind much of our theological segregation. We long to know that life has meaning. We sense that this can be true only as we are related to that which is the source of meaning. We hunger for some contact with the Eternal. But, we are driven by a guilty awareness of our worst natures to define the Almighty as one who could not possibly have any interest in guys like us. Our terrible pride forces us to postulate a God who is beyond the reach of our terrible need.

I have suggested that this seems to be a special problem for men in our time, but no age has been above it. And nowhere is the tragedy more dramatically outlined than in the reaction of Israel to the one whom we call the Christ, in the contrast between messianic expectation and embittered disappointment. To many of the people of his own time Jesus of Nazareth appeared as the symbol of Israel's hope, the focus of their passionate anticipation. Probably no two of the persons whose lives he touched would have defined their expectations in exactly the same way. For some he was to be a militant rebel, liberator of Israel from the yoke of Rome. For others the herald to an end of history and the advent of rule by a celestial bureaucracy. For a few a teacher of great wisdom, whose learning in the law and skill in debate would set straight the confused minds of men. And for many the worker of mighty deeds of healing, one by whom the blind would be given sight and the lame made to walk.

Jesus was the symbol of widely diverse hopes, the focus of passionate expectations. But he was the fulfillment of none of these. His coming among men was a moment of truth, the point at which dream and fact had either to come together like the two pictures in a stereopticon viewer to show reality in new and deeper perspective, or so blur the outlines of conflicting images that men would be confused and angered by the distortion of their visions. In Christ the people of Israel had a chance to change the focus of imagination and see an old myth in a new dimension.

But once again the abstraction, the hope, proved too solidly outlined, too filled in with subjective detail to blend with fact. Jesus was crucified. Not because of any evil that was in him. Not even because of the good that was in him. But because he had come among them and "not as a stranger." For men can tolerate the wholly alien more easily than that which resembles them enough to challenge the veracity of their own profiles. The Holy One of God, they cried, must be exalted. The Messiah must be above the ground upon which we stand, the dust of which we are made. And he *will* be high and lifted up, if we have to nail him there ourselves!

So spoke Israel long ago. But there is enough of that in each of us to say, Amen. Amen and amen. Let it be done. Let us put an end to this desecration of the Eternal, this vulgar, primitive yearning for some condescension by God. If our consciences are troubled at the sound of the consenting echo, we can always repent at the foot of the unadorned cross, that antiseptic symbol of an abstract hope.

And here the matter might rest. Except that having confronted, however briefly and unwillingly, the image of a suffering God, a God who himself bleeds and dies; having confronted this we are never able to get the picture completely out of our minds. Even if we deny all the standard doctrines of the atonement, even if we continue to scoff at the dramatic myths surrounding Calvary and the rending of the temple veil; the Christ we reject in Matthew, Mark, Luke, and John keeps confronting us in the most unlikely places. In Dostoevski, in Camus, in Faulkner, and in the faces of countless men and women who have shed their blood in all the conflicts of history that we might have life and have it more abundantly. Then, we must either deride them all, counting their suffering the ultimate folly, or find some place for it in the pattern of our own thoughts.

Once a man has confronted the suffering God, he begins to see himself in a new light. He becomes able to accept the vulgar, passionate, and torn and bleeding part of his own being that had always seemed somehow unworthy of his best definition of man. He is able to see himself as a whole of which every part has equal dignity. At last he can admit the grandeur of tragedy, that tragedy which had always seemed to be the bitter joke of history at the expense of his finitude.

Having confronted the suffering God, you and I begin to understand where we live. Not on cloud nine, not in the realm of pure reason, not at the summit of a categorical imperative. But on the hill Mizar, among the cedars of Lebanon, and in the ragged tents of those improbable people the Hermonites. We see ourselves as we are: creators of profound thoughts, high hopes, and bright dreams; but bondsmen also of hunger, pain, lust, and fear. And we know that when we pray from platform and pulpit our language may be that of Shakespeare and Milton and the dignified cadences of Cranmer. But in our hearts the substance of our prayers is what men have prayed through all the dusty reaches of time. O God, it hurts. Take away the pain. O God, it's dark. Send us light. O God, she's gone. Give her back to me.

And we pray this way, not because we expect the heavens to open up and straightway make all as we have asked, but because we are powerless *not* to pray this way. For we know who we are, and there is something in our relationship with God which tears such prayers from us against every protest of reason. We know that our hunger and fear, our pain and need to be loved are as much parts of us as the most exalted imagination of our minds. The image of the suffering God makes it possible for us to accept the unity of what we are.

Once a man has accepted this, he comes to understand that no contact between the finite and the infinite is possible without some vulgarization of God. No potter, whatever his skill, can form even the most exquisitely delicate vessel without getting clay on his hands. If God were to touch only the fingertips of our highest and best, "E'en then would be some stooping." * And if our God, like Browning's duke, chose "never to stoop," we would be without hope. God loves us where we are or not at all.

Men in our time are troubled by the religion of the Bible. By the way in which it shuttles back and forth between cosmos and province, by its mixture of theology and geology. And they always will be. For it speaks of the most profound of all mysteries, the way in which the Eternal moves among and touches the lives of men. It is the biography of that classical Christian affirmation, "In the beginning was the Word, . . . and the Word became flesh and dwelt among us (John 1:1, 14)."

---

* Robert Browning, *The Complete Poetic and Dramatic Works of Robert Browning* (Boston: Houghton Mifflin Co., 1895), p. 252.

II

6

the good guys
and
the bad guys

Shortly after World War II the editors of a leading Protestant denominational magazine decided that they would designate and honor some American political leader as "Christian Statesman of the Year." Apparently they believed that politicians would vie with one another to win this accolade and that this competition would raise the tone of public life. After much searching of the national scene and their own souls, these conscientious men selected the governor of one of our southern states, a man notorious for his leadership of the forces of racial segregation. The editors explained their choice in these terms: the governor neither drinks nor smokes and will not serve liquor in his official residence.

I am not concerned at the moment with the propriety of choosing as "Christian Statesman" a man who had served as the high priest of white supremacy. The absurdity of such an act is obvious. My interest here lies in the reason given for honoring this particular politician. *He neither drinks nor smokes* and refuses to serve liquor in his official residence.

This sort of reasoning troubles me because it is typical of a great deal of Protestant thought and reflects a deeply rooted American myth. It assumes that all social, economic, and political phenomena have no significance in themselves and can only be analyzed and evaluated in terms of the conformity of particular individuals to a narrow and provincial morality. Those Protestant editors did not stand alone. A leader of Moral Rearmament announced in the thirties that Adolf Hitler could not be as bad as he was reported to be, since he was known to be both a teetotaler and a vegetarian. A popular mid-western preacher proclaimed his political views in these words: "I ask one thing first about any candidate for public office, Is he a regular reader of the Bible?" The president of a patriotic women's organization announced on network television not long ago that she could never vote for any Presidential candidate who came from a city of over 500,000 people. "They are inevitably," she said, "tainted by the sinks of iniquity from which they arise."

There is something pathetic about such people. They obviously feel a keen responsibility to make ethical judgments about public affairs, to apply their Christian faith to the complex processes of social change. But their efforts to do so are ludicrously irrelevant to the issues with which they are trying to deal. (Hitler was a demonic force in spite of his dietary habits, and Winston Churchill was one of the truly creative leaders of the free world, although he was a notorious drinker and smoked like a chimney.) Their fumbling moralism says as much or more about their common religious background as it does about their individual intelligence.

It is important to understand what produces such sincere irrelevance, because the vice is widespread among Christians and makes a mockery of their ethical witness. People who feel some significant attraction to the gospel are very often turned off by the social, or one might better say antisocial, attitudes of its spokesmen. And the mythology in which this naiveté has its origins works with great subtlety upon the minds of all of us who share the American-Protestant ethos.

The colonization of this continent occurred during an era in which Europe was gripped strongly by three convulsive forces: the Renaissance, the emergence of capitalism, and the Protestant Reformation. All of these had at least one theme in common, the rebellion of the individual against entrenched institutions. In its own way each of them contributed to an intense individualism, the conviction that man achieves stature and fulfillment as he stands *against* the structures of his society. All three helped to compose the mythology with which I am concerned in this discussion. But more than the other two the Protestant Reformation is responsible for the incurable moralism, the romantic social irrelevance of the average American mind.

This is true for several reasons. In the first place the Reformation broke a priestly monopoly on theological and moral discourse. During the unchallenged dominance of Rome, religious speculation was held to be the province of trained theologians, not the right of every man in the street. And the scheme of salvation which was acknowledged by almost all Christians before the Reformation required no individual theological initiatives. Laymen accepted the authority and sacraments of the church with little dissent.

With the appearance of the reformers, however, came also the doctrine of the priesthood of *all* believers. Men were told that they themselves could have direct access to God and needed no ordained intermediary. They were encouraged to read the Bible and learn from it those things essential to the Christian life.

It is not difficult to see what this teaching would contribute to an emerging individualism. The church and her sacraments had always been strong bonds of human interdependence. They had symbolized and ritualized the need of men for one another. When these symbols were dropped, the priesthood of all believers proclaimed, and the right of personal interpretation of scripture asserted, there began to appear a spiritual rationalization for the cultural and economic individualism growing out of the Renaissance and capitalism.

Now it is necessary to point out here that the greatest of the reformers did not state their doctrines in the terms in which I have been describing them. Men like Luther and Calvin had grave reservations about carrying their basic beliefs to the extremes to which they have been taken by others. But popular attitudes are rarely precise. They are shaped by vulgarization not scholarship. Many a prudent rebel has lived to see his carefully articulated views turned into simplistic slogans by more passionate men.

The new individualism which grew out of the Reformation was never able to reach its logical extremes in Europe itself. Deeply laid social patterns were too powerful to be wiped off the map by the virulent new spirit. But America proved to be the most fertile ground possible for the planting of such seed. Here was a vast wilderness, devoid of social structure, tradition, and community. This was an empty land in which men were forced to rely on themselves once they left the huddled colonies of the east coast. They carried their society on their backs and their law on their hips. And built an empire.

So the American myth emerged, sired by the theology of individualism and born of a virgin wilderness. Is there any wonder that it has come to seem of divine origin?

Life in America rapidly grew more complex. Forest gave way to fortress, and fortress became town and then city. The lonely trapper yielded to the long wagon train. Simple social, political, and economic structures were replaced by more complicated ones. Now we are a nation of General Motors, Luce Publications, and Hilton Hotels. Individualism as a *fact* of daily life has long since ceased to exist; and when pressed to discuss his work, the average American will admit that he has become a cog in the vast machine. Indeed, many of the most violent protests of the young are directed against the dehumanizing effects of regimentation in business and politics. No prudent American would plan his career on the basis of an individualistic philosophy of history today.

But when men stop to reflect morally upon the state of the world and try to make ethical decisions for their society, they continue to be influenced by the myths which they have so clearly abandoned for all other purposes. Those who are the most sophisticated operators within the system where their own advancement is concerned frequently remain the victims of an outmoded mythology when they discuss the relationship of religion to business and politics.

This is not surprising. Cultural myths operate largely at the unconscious level. Thus, they can be amended or abrogated in those areas in which they are clearly irrelevant without losing their potency in other respects. In fact, given the semisacred character of folklore, a man who abandons one facet of the traditional mythology for practical reasons is likely to be driven by feelings of guilt and betrayal to cling the more loyally to it where he can do so without loss. Thus, as the necessities of modern social change force Americans to reject many of the canons of individualism in practice, their devotion to them in theory becomes almost fanatical. (Like the unfaithful husband who compulsively tells his friends what a wonderful woman his wife is!)

So it is that when Americans foregather as good Christians or Jews to discuss their social responsibilities, they tend to forget all that they know about the real world and talk in the most simplistic terms about their ethical obligations. In such conclaves they are priests of the myth, sworn to uphold it, wherever practical, at all costs!

The central feature of the individualistic mythology can be briefly stated: society does not really exist. It is a figment of the socialist imagination, a shadow cast on the stage of history by individuals who happen to be standing too close together.

Life magazine, in an article published some years ago, called attention to this phenomenon. Its author was contrasting the characters of the Japanese and American people. The Japanese, he said, think of themselves primarily in their social roles. A man is a son, husband, father, employee, neighbor, soldier, and so on. His personality is the composite of these various relationships. And he imagines that if some mysterious chemistry were to dissolve them, there would be nothing left at all. The American, on the other hand, sees himself as a core personality which from time to time and for limited purposes must play at being a son, husband, father, employee, soldier, and so on. And *he* imagines that if some mysterious chemistry were to dissolve these relationships, it would be a darned good thing.

I know too little about Japan to evaluate this description of its national temper. But the interpretation of the American mood is basically sound. Perhaps the best place to look for evidence of this view of things is in the artifacts of our popular culture. For nothing more vividly delineates what the people of any time and place believe about themselves than those stories and songs and poems and plays which they repeat endlessly with minor variations.

In America the essence of this popular culture is not hard to find. It is distilled for us in "the western," the saga of the frontier and the men who allegedly subdued it. The western may appear as a play, a novel, a movie, or a television drama. But one theme runs through all of its forms, i.e., the impotence of social order and the reliance of the community upon the courage of the lonely hero.

A typical western begins with some town in trouble. The bad guys who were sent to prison a few years ago have been released and are about to descend upon those who put them away. A band of hostile Indians is in the vicinity and out for blood. Trail-weary cowboys have had too much to drink and are planning to burn down the main street. The threats vary, but the response of the town is constant. It trembles helplessly before whatever impends. Those who should organize its resources and direct its defense are unavailable or unwilling to lead. The sheriff is a coward; the cavalry has been called into the hills by false smoke signals; the banker is hiding in the vault with his money bags; and the preacher is at home preparing a dramatic sermon on infant damnation. The "danger music" grows more obvious, and all seems lost.

Then at the critical moment a lonely figure appears at one end of the long, dusty, main street of town. He ties his horse in front of the saloon, slaps some of the alkali from his clothes, and steps up to the bar for a drink. He has no intention whatever of getting involved in this community. It is of the essence of the story that this man is a transient, one who just happens to be passing through en route to some other place and destiny. But something catches his interest. Perhaps one of the villains kicks a dog, a small boy looks trustingly into his face, or an old woman reminds him of his mother. And before he knows it he has agreed to get the town out of whatever trouble it fears.

His method of operation is also standard. He rarely makes any effort to organize the citizenry in their own defense. Such an undertaking would clearly be doomed at the outset. He simply warns innocent bystanders to get out of the way, meets the enemy in the middle of the street, guns him down, then goes on with his interrupted journey. He may be the Lone Ranger, the Texan, the Bounty Hunter, the Restless Gun, Paladin, or one of the boys from *Bonanza*. But his modus operandi is the same in any case. And so is the inference to be drawn from his popularity.

For millions of Americans society does not exist for any practical purposes, except to weaken and corrupt those who depend upon it. The lonely hero is courageous and competent precisely because he is *not involved* in the corrosive social processes which engulf and destroy personal character. The fact that he enters the scene just in time to do what needs doing and leaves immediately thereafter makes this point crystal clear. And as if to underscore it for those too dimly lit to see for themselves, there repeatedly appears in such stories the "ex-hero," i.e., the paunchy rancher or marshall who "used to be" brave and free, until he sold out for marriage, a family, and a position in the community.

Generations of Americans were raised on such myths. Even the children of today's more sophisticated media are seeing them represented, with intriguing variations, many times a week on their television screens. The fact that the message conflicts with other messages enshrined in different myths has not kept it from influencing the world view of countless growing minds. It is the nature of mythology to make little of consistency.

Is there any evidence that the good guy-bad guy conception of history has any real influence on the way people think and act? A great deal. In the realm of politics, for example, it is reflected in the average American's worship of "independence." As a people we are extremely reluctant to affiliate ourselves with one of the major parties; we take great pride in splitting our tickets and tend to find irresistible the candidate who lambastes his own organizational leaders. Amid the complexities of modern government, millions of Americans are obviously looking for the Lone Ranger, the hero who has remained insulated against the compromises and corruptions of politics and will thus be able to vindicate their cause with no inhibiting weaknesses.

Dwight D. Eisenhower's chief claim to the Presidency lay in the fact that he was "not a politician." Senator Eugene McCarthy rallied millions to his cause with a charm composed, in significant part, of his disdain for party policy. And John Lindsay is criticized for switching political camps, because such a move implies the importance of partisan labels.

But perhaps the most clear-cut illustration of our commitment to the good guy-bad guy view of human events can be found in the phenomenal popularity of Gen. Douglas MacArthur during the latter days of the Korean War. The war in Korea, much like the one in Viet Nam, saw the United States bogged down in what seemed a hopeless campaign of unending torment. It was a "police action" or "limited conflict." Our armies were prevented by our diverse international responsibilities from carrying the war to the enemy's home ground. Men died day after day in what seemed often to be a military charade.

Then up spoke General MacArthur. Let us, he said in effect, cut loose from the complex international commitments and timid allies who fetter our arms and "head 'em off at Eagle Pass" (the Yalu River), the way Teddy Roosevelt did at San Juan Hill. Americans can take care of themselves when they stand on their own feet and refuse to be inhibited by the equivocations of diplomacy.

And the nation went wild with enthusiasm. This was the solitary hero, appearing at the head of that long, dusty street ready to rescue the town from its fearful paralysis. MacArthur made what amounted to a triumphal procession across the continent when President Truman summoned him to Washington. And there was much talk of impeaching the chief executive for his unfaithfulness to the American myth.

The roster of Lone Rangers who have captured the hearts of a romantic people is long. It includes sincere men of high purpose and calculating rogues. But all testify to the national conviction that the dynamic of history is the courage of the individual, preferably unfettered by social responsibility. Society is, indeed, unreal and cannot be taken seriously in moral discourse.

The basis of this world view is, you see, the reduction to absurdity of a simplistic Reformation theology. If the grace of God works directly upon *individuals* in what might be called a *vertical* fashion, then the only way God's will can be made applicable to history is through the dedication of those who have come to know him personally. Since there are no Christian criteria for judging the nonexistent social process, one must make his moral decisions by finding out what the good guys are saying and doing and follow their lead.

But how does one tell the good guys from the bad guys without a theological scorecard? Well, one examines a man's private life. If he follows the basic maxims of Christian morality in his dealings with family and friends; avoids the sins of drinking, fornication, and stealing; and attends church or synagogue with reasonable regularity, obviously he is a *good* guy. What could be simpler? It's unfortunate if he stands for racial segregation, national isolation, nuclear war threats, or starvation payments to welfare cases. But all those things are politics, not morality. And so we get the high priest of white supremacy named "Christian Statesman of the Year" by a group of conscientious Christian editors.

Now we come to the real tragedy behind all this pathos. Most of us are not fools. We know that society is real. We have to come to terms with it scores of times every day, make judgments based upon its rules and regulations, and compromise our personal standards in order to live with other men and women. No matter how fervently we may assent to the mythology of individualism in moral discourse, in our hearts we know it's wrong. And we almost inevitably develop a profound contempt for a religion which connives in perpetuating it. We cannot help but resent the religious schizophrenia implicit in this relationship, the division of our consciences and lives into the realm of social realism on the one hand and private morality on the other. We probably go on paying lip service to the myth and its "spiritual" rationalization. However, both our citizenship and our religion suffer from the charade. In time we are likely to make a clean break and abandon all pretense of relating our faith to our daily lives. Thus, Christianity becomes a ritualistic vocabulary, and the real basis of our ethics is the will to survive in a complicated society.

What is the fallacy underlying this good guy-bad guy view of history? It is the assumption that the world is merely a stage on which individuals act out the drama of their personal salvation and that God is concerned with *intentions* not results.

There is no warrant for such a position in the Bible. If the scriptures make anything clear it is that God cares *what* happens in history. In his dealings with the sons of men he is not concerned with their morality as an end in itself but as a *means* by which they may more fully serve his purposes for the world. The Holy One is constantly giving the people of Israel very explicit directions about the conduct of their common life. They are told what to eat, drink, and wear. They are told where to live and when to go there. Their economic, political, and domestic relationships are defined and governed down to the most minute detail.

In the process of getting things done, God does not hesitate to use men of mixed character and motives, men who violate not only the commandments but even the dictates of common decency. It is impossible to imagine that the God of Abraham, Isaac, and Jacob cared more about the personal virtues of Moses than he did about the liberation of his captive people.

When one turns to the New Testament, the same lesson is spelled out in various ways. Jesus Christ came among men that "the *world* through him might be saved"; not a group of clean Christian athletes, but "the *world*." And when Jesus told his followers the story of the Great Judgment he said that "the *nations*" would be called before the throne for final disposition. The *nation* which fed the hungry, visited the sick, and freed the oppressed would be saved. And the *nation* which did not do these things would be cast into the fires of hell. This is not an argument for Christian socialism. It is an affirmation that God cares about what *happens* to his people and not simply about the strengths and weaknesses of well-meaning individuals.

This is by no means to argue that personal virtues are without significance. They are obviously important parts of the dynamic of history and taken together have an immeasurable influence upon what occurs at any time or place. But their significance is something to be evaluated in the context of events and judged by their contribution to the results which God wills.

The best Christian thought has never been willing to ignore the fact of human interdependence. It understands, indeed insists, that the Lone Ranger is as phoney theologically as he is historically. For it remembers the words of the psalmist, "The earth is the Lord's and the fullness thereof; the world and they that dwell therein (Ps. 24:1)."

7
artists and the real world

Several years ago on the weekend preceding Lent the students of the Yale Divinity School held an ambitious and well-organized Arts Festival. They brought in speakers from various departments of the university, borrowed a selection of controversial paintings, presented experimental musical compositions, and produced plays by Becket and Ionesco. For three days we all reveled in culture.

As I lived amid these events, surrounded by striking colors, shapes, sounds, and happenings, I found myself thinking with some amusement of how startled my faculty predecessors of fifty years ago would have been by what was taking place in the divinity quadrangle. (The students had the grace to veil the portraits in the Common Room.)

But when the amusement had worn off, I began to wonder quite seriously *why* our Protestant forebears viewed the arts with the deep suspicion which characterized their attitude toward them. Why did the great frontier evangelist Charles Finney, first President of Oberlin College, refer to all dramatists and actors as "a host of triflers and blasphemers of God of whom William Shakespeare was the chief"? Why did Dwight L. Moody, founder of two of the nation's best preparatory schools, regard fiction and poetry as morally dangerous and to be tolerated only when they were intended to make graphic the wages of sin? And how can we account for the fact that even some of the more radical academic theologians of the recent past treated theater-going and popular songsinging as mere extensions of those quaint biblical vices "chambering and wantonness"?

As difficult as it is for young people of this generation to understand, however, American Christians, including Roman Catholics who in this matter seem to have come quickly under the spell of Protestant mores, until a very few years ago tended to equate works of art with works of the devil.

The reasons for this distrust are, of course, numerous. And for the most part they reflect more discredit upon religion than upon art. The fear that the mirror held up to nature might, as so many other mirrors have done, conduce to vanity was undoubtedly an important force in shaping such attitudes. Anything which turns man's attention toward the world around him, anything which

---

This chapter was published originally as "The Aesthetic Heresy" in *Reflection,* Vol. 66, No. 1, Nov. 1968. Reprinted by permission.

makes life interesting, exciting, and worthy of speculation, and anything which focuses human curiosity upon the depth dimension of history can be accused of undermining the piety of an otherworldly faith. Obviously, much of the hostility of eighteenth- and nineteenth-century churches toward aesthetic experiences reflected an antilife theology which we are fortunate to have outgrown.

But there is a sense, is there not, in which the artistic enterprises participate in and perhaps even epitomize the human rebellion against God and thus threaten the health of the human personality. Surely one cannot affirm that while all other forms of human activity, politics, business, sex, scholarship, science, and so on, one cannot affirm that while all of these reflect in distinctive ways the corruption of man, the aesthetic vitalities alone are for some strange reason beyond the reach of sin. Like every other manifestation of mortal energy, artistic impulses can become the media of self-destruction and the corruption of others. The artist is, with all the rest of us, descended from Adam, "that first man whose fall brought sin and death into the world," and he must, therefore, walk with other men the narrow, common path between creative freedom and destructive rebellion. It may well be that the demonic possibilities of genius are in direct proportion to its constructive potential.

There are many ways in which the content of this allegation might be explicated. For me the root of the danger lies in the ability of the artist to manipulate the component elements of life in what *can* be an ultimately irresponsible fashion, the complete control which he enjoys over both the internal development of his creatures and the context in which that development takes place.

Let me illustrate what I mean:

When a man purports to record history, and I use that phrase in the broadest sense to include all media of expression, what he sets down is subject to various kinds of confirmation or rebuttal. If one alleges that Louis XVI was a genius at statecraft, Josef Stalin a great humanitarian, or Marilyn Monroe a withered hag, we can adduce abundant evidence to make him out a fool, a liar, or some kind of exotic deviate! History is populated by enough objective data and subject to sufficient consensus to make relatively useful judgments possible, although surely not easy.

But when we turn from history to art, the situation is radically altered. So far as his own creatures are concerned the artist is a god. He is the master of both character and continuity. He can tell us that John Doe spent his life in profligate self-indulgence, brutally exploited his senses, and plundered his neighbors; but digested his food perfectly, slept well every night, and raised three fine children who worshiped their father, joined the Peace Corps, and set an example to all who knew them. The playwright can, and often does, portray people who combine virtues and vices in piquant, winsome patterns never achieved in real life. He can make villains exciting and good men dull, rakehells full of compassion and faithful husbands objects of ridicule. The painter can present the human form so splendidly beautiful or hideously deformed that the viewer's psyche is beguiled or traumatized by what he sees. In short, the artist can mix and match the component elements of life in unrealistic and even irresponsible ways.

I remember reading an article by a physicist who had served briefly as technical consultant to a science-fiction series on television. It was his job to lend an atmosphere of fact to what was essentially fantasy. He reported that one day he was given a script which called for the hero to be on Earth one afternoon and on Mars early the next morning. The chronology troubled him, and he spent some time trying to work out the vocabulary by which the feat might be accomplished. Finally the director took him off the hook. "Oh, don't worry about that," he said. "We'll just fade out on Earth that afternoon and cut back in on Mars the next morning."

Well, this is a marvelous arrangement, isn't it? Fade out this side of the problem of human finitude and cut back in just beyond it.

You may be disposed at this point to object and say, "Oh, come now." Except for the purest fantasy, the people in even a bad book or a poor play do live in our world. What they are supposed to feel, say, and do can be measured by many yardsticks of equivalent or analogous experience and valid judgments made as to the authenticity of what is said about them.

This may have been true at one time. But is it true today? Our age feels considerable embarrassment about holding the mirror up to nature, about tying imagination to some discernible relationship to fact. The integrity of a work of art, we are told now, must not be tested by its resemblance to something identifiable in the external world, by the degree to which it speaks in the vulgar tongue. The watchword is, What does it mean to you? And it need not mean to you what it means to him or her, or me. Indeed, we are warned by those who instruct us in the raising of our children that when a youngster brings home some tinted, textured ambiguity, we must on no account ask, What is it? But must simply interact with whatever is put before us as though the world of rocks and trees, flesh and blood, and life and death were very largely a matter of personal opinion.

Now I know from sad experience that by that last paragraph I have in the minds of many forever categorized myself as the implacable foe of all contemporary modes of aesthetic expression. A man can stand before a university audience and proclaim the disintegration of sexual standards, the need for a radical revision in our economy, the bankruptcy of American foreign policy, and even the death of God and be carried from the hall on the shoulders of an admiring throng. But let him suggest that the world of creative imagination is as deeply involved in the general corruption of man as any other area of life and the "amens" quickly turn to "O Gods."

But the fact that this is true, the fact that so many intellectuals will brook no criticism of contemporary modes of nonrepresentational art illustrates dramatically the very point of my argument. Human pride, the determination to transcend and deny mortality can turn even the most precious of gifts, creativity, into a potent weapon of depravity.

You see, the great artist is always torn between what is his personal vision of the world around him and those unrefined generalizations which he shares with all men, between life as he is given the power to see it by the peculiar complex of experience and skill which makes up his personality and the grosser outlines of reality which bounce off all human eyes and ears in much the same way. One might put this in another form and say that the artist is forever in rebellion against the limitations of the vernacular, forever at war with his listener-viewer's poverty of experience, imagination, and symbolism. Or at war simply with the public otherness, the immutable fact that men have different and often incompatible stores of response and language.

Now all authentic creativity consists of living somehow with that tension, of giving expression to what is one's own without losing touch with what one shares with the race. The truly great artist is the one who manages in one way or another to stay en rapport with his vision *and* his humanity. This is a terrible and painful balance to sustain. And because it is both important and difficult, it is here that pride strikes most often and with the most devastating effect.

Be true to yourself, it urges. Admit once and for all that your *self* is most truly present in your uniqueness. You are not really the earthbound creature who has one hand always clasped by the clammy palm of fellowship. You, pride insists, are enshrined in your particularity. That is your essence. And it follows, therefore, as the night the day that you are being most true to yourself when you reject finally and completely the demands of every other.

We are told in the book of Genesis that Adam was given by God the task of naming all created objects, that whatever Adam called anything, *that* became its name. This suggests, does it not, that the very foundation of religion is the power to look at some external reality and say, That is a bird, a rock, a tree. And it has both existence and significance which are independent of my subjective response. Oh, because I am something special, the like of which in common with its fingerprints has never been before nor ever will be again; I see that bird, that rock, that tree in slightly special ways, with shades, shadows, and proportions which are gifts of my own eye. But this is the mere upper edge of sight, God's concession to my uniqueness and then in turn my gift of myself to other men.

But if in a spasm of conceit I take in hand a pen, a brush, or flute and print upon your eye or weave around your ear the merest upper edge of what I see, the outer rim of what I hear, ignoring what we see and hear in common, I have made truth my own gift to me and a principle of division between us. For now I call *most real* what I alone possess and you can never share.

The most significant and damning kind of atheism does not consist of negative sentences containing the word "God." It consists, rather, of the allegation that reality is wholly defined by my vision and subject to total manipulation at my convenience. And it is this kind of atheism in the shadow of which human creativity always stands. Man is forever tempted to use his highest gifts to fabricate worlds which exist only in his own mind, worlds in which he is God and makes all the rules.

To say that the artist is in special danger of this kind of corruption is, of course, to affirm the grandeur of his role in history. It is to recognize that he is dealing with truth more intimately than most men ever can and that when he loses contact with the common life it is often a kind of self-sacrifice, the risk of his own soul in the effort to reach some insight which lies beyond the length of his mortal arm.

This, however, is the very essence of human sinfulness. Men have often been damned by their own best intentions: by power which they sought initially for laudable purposes; by passion which was the first fruit of love; by fear which began as tender sensitivity to the feelings of others. And men can be damned by creative aspiration which turns into presumption, pride, and the final denial of *the other*. A man can try so hard to reach the unique truth which lies deep in the well of his own being that he loses his balance, falls in, and drowns.

We are naturally reluctant to admit this hard fact of life. Most of us are neurotically defensive about the purity of contemporary art, because any attack upon the integrity of the artist's subjectivity is at the same time an attack upon the possibility of a redeeming detachment. We live in a world in which external reality impinges more and more demandingly upon us. Day by day the options become less varied, the channels of freedom narrower. Other lives, other hopes, and other needs increasingly prescribe the boundaries and conditions of our existence. So we long to believe in the possibility of an internal sovereignty and look for cabalistic formulas which will give us ultimate control or final immunity from the structures of fact around us. The artist who claims, or appears to claim, that reality is fully encompassed in his own subjectivity becomes our champion against that representationalism which alleges the immutability of the moral context.

So we refuse to distinguish between the artist who reluctantly lets go of the vernacular in his zeal to reach the truth and the faker who happily flees the vernacular in order to avoid the truth. Indeed, the latter is often the most eagerly endowed with our blessing, because what we so often want from art is not truth but the very refuge from truth which the artist sometimes seeks on our behalf.

Some time ago I saw a painting which was titled "The Brokenness of Man." It was a splendidly abstract thing, a complex of lights, shadows, jagged angles, and broken lines. It was so powerful that I wanted to stand and look at it for a long time, or better still take it home and hang it on my wall and invite my friends in to view it, as we sipped coffee and nibbled crackers and cheese. I contemplated the deep discussions which it might stimulate and heard myself saying that it takes a real artist to catch the truth about such things.

Then suddenly I remembered a photograph that I had seen shortly before. It had been taken by a cameraman who specialized in recording the seamy side of New York City and showed a drunk lying unconscious in a Harlem doorway. He had a three-day growth of beard on his face, a shock of unkempt hair, vomit all over his chest, snot running from his nose, and a wine bottle wrapped in brown paper clutched in the crook of an elbow. *This* was a broken man. And I did not linger in front of that portrait. Nor did I long to take it home and hang it on my wall and have my friends in to view it as we sipped coffee and nibbled crackers and cheese. This was a broken man. And all I wanted was to get away from him as rapidly as possible.

We must not, as some are minded to, suppose that when the Great Divorce occurred between heaven and hell God was given unconditional custody of the crayons. Satan gets them on weekends. And he makes good use of his visiting privileges. There is a kind of art which is possessed and not by us. There is an art which while purporting to reveal the truth in new depth by showing it in strange perspectives, so blurs its outlines that men conclude that there is no such thing as truth at all. If we were angels and not mere human beings, we might play loosely with fact and do no harm to truth. But a large part of what it means to be mortal is to be unable to separate fact from truth. Stones are stones and bread is bread. And while some confusion between them *may* be the sign of a special grace, it may also be the prelude to condemnation. There is a shape of things as they are and to be finally alienated from it is Hell. Only God can say, "I am that I am." "It is he that has made us and not we ourselves."

8
the quitters

The modern American is undoubtedly one of the most mobile creatures that the earth has ever produced. Motion is in many respects the primary quality of his existence. I speak now partly as observer, one who has read the literature, examined the statistics, studied the graphs, and watched the spurts and spasms of individual energy blend subtly into the flow of social mobility.

But I speak also as victim, as one whose life is filled with fragments, half-remembered friends, gardens abandoned before the seeds had sprouted, empty rooms echoing the voices of the mover's men, while I stared at the corner where my bed had stood or reached out to touch a light spot on the wall from which a favorite picture had just been removed. Like most of you I have too often closed a door and said to myself as I did so, "I am closing it now for the last time, and a tiny fraction of my life will be forever shut inside."

The problem manifests itself most obviously, of course, in spatial terms. We move from place to place with great frequency and even greater rapidity. In the process we manage to commit various forms of mayhem upon ourselves and our fellow travelers. Long hours spent in long lines on long journeys have written the story of physical mobility upon our faces. Individual and mass transportation have given us the ability to live in one community, work in another, send our children to school in a third, and enjoy open or furtive recreations in a fourth. All this occurs with little more effort than it takes to press an accelerator.

In social terms we are almost equally mobile. The old Horatio Alger myth is a somewhat less accurate reflection of the facts of life than it used to be. But it still bears a recognizable resemblance to the truth. We move up and down various ladders of wages, status, fringe benefits, and acceptance in a manner largely conditioned by talent and motivation. The fact that this is the case with most of us is what creates deep resentment in those who for reasons of race or parental poverty are excluded from the ladder.

And, finally, we are the possessors of a high degree of psychological mobility. A man or woman sitting in a dingy hall bedroom can by the magic of television be lifted out of his immediate surroundings and carried into the councils of state, the homes of the famous and notorious, or a world of romantic adventure. The poor devil who does not rate a second glance from the shop foreman or the attractive blond at the next desk often finds himself chatting amiably with the President of the United States or being seduced visually by Hollywood's reigning starlet.

Now clearly the composite of these mobilities has great appeal for any normal human being. It lets us mix and match the component elements of our daily lives. We can live where the grass is green, work where the prospects are golden, and send the kids to school where their classmates are socially acceptable. Lawns, shopping centers, theaters, and friends are within easy reach, as well as those windows upon the great world through which we can at least see what we do not actually possess. In a far more complete way than has ever been possible before, men in our time can have the best of many worlds rolled into one.

It would be the worst form of pious cant to pretend that mobility is wholly and inherently evil. Up to a certain point it is both a material and moral blessing. Many forms of human corruption thrive on provincialism. The man who spends all of every day of his life trapped in one community, repeating endlessly the same routines in company with the same people, hearing the familiar stories, singing the old refrains, steeping himself in ancient prejudices, frequently tends to absolutize the traditional and make a virtue of monotony. It is no wonder that the little old ladies in sneakers hate the United Nations with slobbering passion, for it symbolizes a real world that goes on beyond the end of the local bus line. The love of God can and does act creatively, judgmentally, and redemptively in the ability of men in our time to see and go into new and strange places.

But man being the sinner that he is, the grace of mobility is inevitably corrupted and becomes the tool of human betrayal and degradation. You and I begin to believe that if we just make policy properly, we can have everything. We lose track of what it means to be finite, which is to say, we forget that we are earthborn creatures, conceived in the union of particular parents, sheltered in the confines of a specific home, fed, protected, and educated by the processes and structures of historical communities, and bearing upon our persons the marks of identification put there by acts of discipline and tenderness on the part of people whose names we can no longer remember. Our mobility tempts us to suppose that we can wholly transcend those mortal limits which have shaped and often warped the lives of lesser generations.

Thus we set about building social, economic, and even religious structures which have their foundations not upon the ground of reality but in the realm of taste, preference, and whim. We gather friends for particular purposes, qualities, and gifts. We choose the best bridge players, the ones whose children get along with our own, those whose skills or possessions fill some gap in our own arsenal, the men whose views on current issues echo faithfully those articulated at our breakfast table, or the women who fit conveniently into the nursery school car pool. We come together with these people for definite purposes and limited periods. Then we separate before they can enmesh us in those aspects of their lives which are less to our liking.

"Tommy said that Mrs. Roberts had been crying when she picked them up at school this afternoon. I do hope nothing's wrong at their house. It would be awfully hard to work things out on Thursdays what with Cubs and Brownies. If we didn't have that station wagon. . . . Ed's been drinking more than he can handle lately. We're going to have to get another couple for the bridge club, if that keeps up."

Do those statements seem a bit extreme? They are word for word quotations from conversations in which I have been involved very recently.

Have generations of philosophers and theologians fretted about the problem of evil? It's no problem for us modern Americans. Just put the kids in the car and hit the road. Is there corruption in local politics? Move. Are the schools falling apart under an overload of children? Move. Have ethnic and racial conflicts begun to spring up around the fringes of the neighborhood? Move. The anthem of mobility rings out over hill and dale:

> Is there trouble and temptation?
> Is there sorrow anywhere?
> We need never be discouraged.
> No one's making us stay there.

Now in fairness one must admit that our consciences are not entirely easy in this matter. We sense unhappily that fellowship cannot be all take and no give, that there are larger purposes to be served by society than our personal convenience and pleasure. So in response to this understanding, we form a multitude of organizations which have as their avowed purpose "service to the community." We foregather every first Monday or third Thursday at some local hostelry or hall, where we sing songs about the social utility of cheerfulness and hear talks about the cheerfulness of social utility. We join fraternal orders and periodically don plumed hats and fringed aprons and sober looks as we recite liturgies of total dedication to some cosmic abstraction. If political problems seem to demand our attention, we organize reform movements, meet in someone's living room two weeks before an election, and compose a letter to the press in which we denounce corruption in government. Sometimes we do none of these things and simply retreat from the big, bad, real world into a realm of telefantasy in *City Hospital* or *Cimmaron Strip*.

The nice thing about our service clubs and fraternal orders is that they are so tidy. They enable us to gather all of our responsibilities into a single package which we share with other people very much like ourselves, people who are invited to join *because* they are like ourselves, and discharge our sense of obligation under auspices firmly controlled by "our kind." And such involvements are neat in another sense. They permit us to prescribe and severely limit the degree of our participation in the human drama. If one becomes active in partisan politics, a labor union, or even the PTA, he runs the risk of being drawn in more completely than he had ever intended. Such engagements tend to turn controversial, even nasty, and set the telephone ringing at the most inconvenient times!

However, a service club or a fraternal order guarantees to provide the feeling of participation and the liturgies of service without any of the unpleasant side effects so often associated with the real world.

Nicholas Murray Butler once said that our time would be known historically as "the age of limited liability." He was speaking about corporations and their enormous impact upon the economic life of Western civilization. But he spoke a larger truth, didn't he? We are people who have used the grace of mobility to limit the degree of our liability to the human community.

There is, of course, one thing wrong with our cult of detachment, with our confidence in horizontal, vertical, and psychological mobility. We cannot move far enough or fast enough to get away from God, which is just a theological way of saying that the world is real. There are historical structures within which men are created, judged, and redeemed. There are ultimate communities from which no one ever escapes. The community of hunger which extends the right hand of fellowship to us as we walk along city streets. The community of pain which grips our vitals in the middle of the night and whose fraternal greeting we cannot mistake for any other. The community of power; the community of fear; the community of death.

There is a frame of things fashioned by God within which our lives are shaped not by our whim but by his will. We flee urban blight to save our children from contamination. And the slums send their switch-blade ambassadors into our "nice" neighborhoods to speak of boundary disputes that have never been finally settled. We form civic reform movements made up of the best people, and the decisions which shape our common future are often left to the worst people. We gather faithful remnants of piety from all over the city under gothic arches and colonial spires. And in offices, alleys, bars, and brothels, where men are driven by myriad, urgent necessities, the spirit of God may be more truly at work.

I am arguing, you see, that the activity of God establishes its own categories, categories which are not subject to our consent or susceptible to our manipulation. There are limits to human mobility in any given generation which are imposed not by technological data but by the inexorable facts of life. Men who move too often and too fast inevitably generate anxieties which reflect their sense of rootlessness. They complain that they have no "real friends, you know, the kind we used to have when we were young." Their families fall apart or wither from lack of sustaining love. And the world at last becomes for them trackless space in which even movement no longer has meaning.

There *are* limits to human mobility. Sociologists can chart and even measure the degree of openness in any society. But the man who believes that he can cut himself off completely from his origins and move with uninhibited grace across every social spectrum makes a serious error. The one Jew who is invited to join the local country club or the "different" Negro who is tolerated in the neighborhood because he is not like all the others will soon learn that he is far more like the others than he had ever dreamed.

There *are* limits to human mobility. The man who lets himself be too often enchanted by far away places with strange sounding names or the realms of beguiling drama which can become his psychological milieu through the miracles of electronics may one day discover that he has lost touch *with* and taste *for* the opportunities and obligations of the real world.

Mobility can be a kind of grace. It can save us from absolutizing the familiar and defining morality as the monotonous repetition of past mistakes. It can be the means of encountering the richly varied forms which are historical expressions of the will of God.

But mobility can also be the most subtle medium of condemnation, for it encourages us to confuse change with creativity. It blinds us to the eternal in its emphasis upon novelty. And it allows us to look for hope in escape from the lost present rather than in its redemption. Nothing can liberate man from the eternal frame of things. But frequent and frantic movement can rob him of his sense of involvement in that structure. It can make impossible those relationships of deep and continuing responsibility, the stubborn confrontation with the same demanding challenge by which we are compelled to look into ourselves and relate what we find to the world around us. It can prevent us from putting down those roots which, although they go into the earth, really reach toward heaven. The effort of man to have the best of all worlds inevitably ends in his having no world at all.

9
preach what you practice

One of the charges made most often against religious people is the allegation that they do not practice what they preach. This is probably said more often about Christians than about the adherents to the world's other great faiths. Not because Christians are so much worse than nonchristians, but because we do so much preaching and what we preach sets such high standards for human behavior.

Well, no honest Christian will deny the indictment. We do leave undone the things which we should have done and do those things which we should not do. We are a pretty unhealthy crowd, spiritually speaking. When one contrasts the harder facts of life, poverty, injustice, hatred, and fear with the comfort in which most church members live, it is difficult to deny that Christians do not adequately or often practice what they preach. This needs to be said frequently and with conviction.

But there is another side to the whole matter about which men in our time speak very little. And it involves not only professing Christians but a great many nonchristians as well. I am speaking now of the refusal of modern man to *preach* what he *practices*.

At this point you may begin to feel a bit nervous, fearful that I am about to make an appeal for more of what is called "personal evangelism," that I am going to call upon you to buttonhole people on the streets, hand out tracts at the office, and inquire moistly about the exact condition of your neighbor's soul. Well, there may be something to be said for all that. But I am not about to say it.

When I suggest that we do not often enough preach what we practice, I am using the word "preach" in its broadest sense and mean to say that most of us do not often raise for honest evaluation and sharing the basic convictions which really move and guide our lives. I am charging that most modern Christians have let the relationship between faith and practice become an automatic thing, something to be taken for granted and avoided in polite conversation.

For me, one of life's minor ordeals is finding myself sitting on an airplane, facing a four- to five-hour trip, and next to a man who wants to talk, but who wants to talk about nothing but trivialities. A half hour on baseball, football, and the latest scandal in politics can be diverting. An hour is bearable, but five hours of chitchat drives me crazy. So I have learned that the surest, quickest way to end such conversation is to bring up a serious issue and ask my talkative companion about its moral implications. What's wrong about adultery? What's so right about family life and the market economy?

For a few seconds he waits expectantly for the punch line of my little joke. But when he perceives that I am serious and mean to pursue the inquiry, he mutters something appropriate such as, "Well, Jesus," and quickly discovers urgent business in the center spread of *Playboy*. If he is willing to take up the challenge, it is inevitably in terms of the most obvious and irrelevant generalities.

One spring I led a three-day conference at a preparatory school for boys in Connecticut. This involved sitting in on classes in philosophy, religion, literature, and so on, as well as lecturing. At the beginning of the first morning of classes the teacher in charge warned me, "You're going to have a terrible time getting these kids to talk about what *they* really believe personally. They'll try to get you off onto everything else—what Albert Schweitzer thought, what Paul Tillich wrote, what the God-is-dead theologians are saying. But just try to get them to open up about what they think!"

And I found that he was right. As the father of two sons, I had always seemed to hear a good deal about *their* ideas. But I quickly discovered that when you move out of the family circle the atmosphere changes dramatically. Even when I pushed the boys as subtly and as openly, as courteously and as rudely as I could, they would slide away from under the question and end up telling me what "some guy in California," an article in *The New York Times,* or the latest revelation from Simon and Garfunkel said about the issue. Their own convictions, if any, remained veiled.

There are a great many things wrong with refusing to talk about what you believe. But I want here to speak of just three of them.

First, by avoiding discussion of the religious implications of our daily behavior, we manage to avoid facing those implications directly. The man who said that he did not know what he believed about a particular subject because he had never heard himself talk about it spoke a more profound truth than he intended. Nothing forces the organization of ideas as effectively as the need to speak about them. The relationship between thought and language is subtle but profoundly significant. Many of us do not really examine our attitudes until we are called upon to state a position.

Thus, failure to express the assumptions upon which one's actions are based can be the best defense in the world against an honest analysis of those actions. Suppose that you were called upon right now to preach a sermon, for example, using what you did yesterday as a storehouse of illustrations? Would that necessity make you want in any way to go back and live yesterday in a somewhat different fashion? In all likelihood the answer to that question is, Yes. But unless one is asked to do some such improbable thing, and the odds are greatly against it, the occasion to examine the quality of one's routine activities rarely arises.

If, on the other hand, talk about values and motives was as common in the human community today as it has been in some periods of history, the occasion for self-examination of a constructive type would occur often. And such discussion would promote a *kind* of self-examination which would be a lot healthier than the sort of morbidly sneaky peeks which most of us take at our ethics when we think that no one is looking.

The second reason for preaching what you practice is that talking about one's faith can refine and strengthen conviction. Failure to do so may lead to spiritual stagnation and the atrophy of belief. There are a great many men and women whose last serious discussion of theology took place in Sunday school. As such people mature most other aspects of their lives reflect the increasing complexities of adult responsibilities and experience. But their religion remains that of an adolescent, because it is never taken out for examination and compelled to state itself in terms appropriate to greater maturity.

This in itself is sad. Because Sunday school piety, even if it never has to confront a crisis of faith, may tend to narrow and inhibit the broader areas of adult development. However, the real danger of such a situation lies in the inability of adolescent religion to cope with those moral crises to which every life is eventually exposed. Many a man whose gifts and energies have carried him to a position of power in the world of affairs finds his Christianity no help to him in difficult decisions, because it has not grown along with the scope of his responsibility. He may blame himself for having departed from the faith of his parents and generate quite an aggressive set of guilt feelings about his theological defection. But such reactions are usually both unfair and useless. The fault lies not in the inability of the individual to fit an adult life into an adolescent religion, but in the failure to have kept religion growing along with everything else in one's personality.

There are, of course, a number of ways in which religious values can be kept abreast of maturity. One of the best of them is a serious effort to articulate one's convictions vis-à-vis the challenges met in the course of everyday life. Whenever we consciously apply our ideas in any field to practical problem solving, we test and modify the ideas as well as elucidate the area under consideration. Thus, the process of *telling others* why we feel and act as we do in specific situations keeps our theology up to date in the best sense of the phrase, increases its relevance to action, and gives it a more respected place in the structures of our thought.

My third reason for counseling you to preach what you practice has less to do with the inner life of the preacher than with the future form of the world in which we all live. One of the most obvious facts about the twentieth century is that it represents a swift movement of the human community toward planned societies of various kinds. Many nations have already opted for socialism or communism in response to the need for increased management of economic and social change. But many more are feeling their way cautiously along the new road, working on an ad hoc basis from day to day, trying by experimentation to find methods which will assure an optimum combination of stability and freedom.

These countries, and the United States is one of them, are faced with the problem of deciding *by what values* planning is to be done in the years ahead. Certain values immediately suggest themselves and need little or no serious debate. Obviously whatever men do, either individually or collectively, should be done with efficiency, imagination, fairness to all concerned in the programs, and so on. But once one has moved beyond this level of self-evident standards, more profound and delicate issues begin to appear.

Some of these were illustrated in a conversation that I had with a student of city planning recently. Our meeting took place in an upstate New York metropolis where I was lecturing and the young man was doing a project in urban renewal for his graduate degree. He asked me a great many questions about New Haven, because of my home community's notable progress in the area of his interest. When he had finished his inquiry, I asked him a question. "Based on your study," I said, "what do you regard as the greatest unsolved problem in urban development?"

His reply came quickly. "It's a religious problem."

I indicated some impatience with what I took to be a courteous recognition of my own vocational involvement. But he persisted.

"No, I mean it," he continued. "You see what we are trying to do in redevelopment is build 'good' cities. But what is a 'good' city? Obviously it is one in which men and women can lead 'good' lives. Now, what is the 'good' life? That's a religious question, isn't it?"

I had to admit that he was right. And I remembered then many conversations which I had had with city planners in which substantially the same thing has been said in other words. We are being called upon all over the world today to make what are essentially judgments about the good life, the nature of a creative community, and the obligations of rich to poor, white to black, and young to old. Should we, for example, gather all the aged together in so-called golden age housing projects, where they have the advantage of fellowship with their peers? Or is it better to scatter the senior citizens through the various neighborhoods of the city so that they can serve as a balancing factor among young people and give the benefit of their experience to new families just starting out in life? What about the black poor? Scatter them and integrate? Or localize and increase their political bargaining power?

There are no easy answers to these queries. But they cannot be dealt with responsibly without taking into consideration values which are religious in character. The nature and destiny of man is a theological problem. However it is inescapably involved in some very practical decisions facing communities all around us today. The present drift is to have the value judgments of which I have been speaking made automatically by the technicians and planners charged with drawing up blueprints and demographic curves. In one city, for example, the decision about where the aged should live was made by the accident of a grant for senior housing happening to be available at a time when the only piece of land cleared and ready for building was in a central urban area. No one asked, Should older people live there? The dynamics of administrative procedure dictated the choice.

I have used urban renewal merely as an illustration of the massive responsibility facing modern societies as they plan for their futures. But the same issues arise at every level of government and with respect to myriad decisions of a critical kind. The shape of tomorrow is in many ways being determined almost casually by architects, social workers, traffic experts, and their fellow professionals. *Not* because these honest and earnest human beings are trying craftily to dominate the future. But because they are the ones on the spot and are forced to decide by the best measure available to them.

In practical terms this means that planning values are being inferred from the atmosphere in which the planners work. The things that are taken for granted, commonly believed, generally understood, and approved by the body of conventional wisdom—these are what provide the basis for building the cities, states, and nations of the twenty-first century.

It is here, then, that one can see the importance of preaching what one practices as a social virtue. What you and I believe will *not* find its way into the atmosphere simply because we believe it. What is taken for granted, commonly believed, and generally understood is the product of what men *say* about what they do, as well as the deeds themselves. Acts in themselves can argue in various directions. Interpretation is necessary if they are to be taken as manifestations of particular convictions. It is not difficult to see in any community examples of poor planning based upon what might be called inadequate articulation and group conflict which results from the wrong inference from familiar practice. A good deal more preaching is needed, if such errors and conflict are to be minimized.

Once again let me say that I am not suggesting a resurgence of personal evangelism in traditional terms. Nor would I want to see Christians conspiring to propagandize their neighbors in order to revitalize their own faith or dominate the shape of things to come. The challenge is not to force religious discourse upon persons or situations, but to overcome the reluctance to speak one's convictions where every condition makes such expression not only appropriate but necessary. The last thing in the world that any reasonably sophisticated American in our time is likely to do is become offensively zealous in the proclamation of his faith. He is less apt to preach what he practices than he is to practice what he preaches. And the former is almost as bad as the latter.

III

10
the uses of alienation

Several years ago the *New Yorker* carried a cartoon in which two middle-aged women were shown discussing a married couple seated near them in a restaurant. One of the women was saying, "Oh, she's a perfect saint. But, of course, he's much more of a person."

The distinction between saintliness on the one hand and a full human personality on the other is surely not an unfamiliar one. It has been expressed in every age as far back as the record of Christianity runs and has always seemed to strike a responsive chord in the hearts of ordinary men. Most of us suspect, do we not, that the saint is a kind of traitor to the human race, that he is not so much marching to the beat of a different drummer as he is floating along about 6 inches above the ground on which the rest of us set our aching feet, that he has purchased sanctification at the expense of his humanity, and sold out to some loyalty beyond the reach of his mortal commitments. One need not be a cynic to empathize with Mark Twain's description of an acquaintance as "a good man in the worst sense of the word."

On the other hand, there is a tradition almost as old and honored which harbors a sneaking respect for men of evil reputation and women of easy virtue. Sometimes this is expressly stated, albeit in defensive terms. ("Well, he's frank about what he is. There's no pretense in him." Or, "She's not a hypocrite. You have to give her that." And you do.) But more often our favorable reaction to the courageously immoral is implied rather than stated. One must discern its presence and measure its power by reading between the lines of our more familiar pieties.

I am thinking, for example, about the way in which our ambivalence toward virtue reflects itself in the popular culture, the prominence of the antihero in all forms of contemporary fiction. The phenomenon is not entirely new. Outlaws, bandits, pirates, and their like have always provided storytellers with some of their most appealing characters. From Robin Hood to Alexander Mundi, the roster of attractive scamps is a long one and decidedly international in flavor. In recent decades, however, the public adulation of the heel has reached a new volume and the subterfuges with which it used to be justified or explained have been dropped. It is no longer necessary to have the robber take from the rich to give to the poor or confine his predatory attentions to those silly parasites who so richly deserved the loss of the extravagances "liberated" by the gentleman burglar.

Today the movies can present *Alfie* or *The Dirty Dozen* with neither apology nor rationalization. And television offers every week a series of cynical and sexy "heroes" who stand head and shoulders above the mousy citizens upon whose women and wealth they so blithely prey. The moral is too clear to be missed by even the most naïve viewer. Villains are strong, brave, and fascinating individuals. Good people are weak, cowardly, and dull. And just in case anyone is stupid enough to miss the point, there appears in all of the mass media from time to time the clergyman who is depicted as the quintessence of everything that you would not want your daughter to marry.

These images are so frequently repeated in our contemporary mythology that one cannot escape the conclusion that they represent a widely held, deeply believed conviction about life itself. However far the representations of fiction may be from reality as scholars understand it, the heroes, villains, and themes of movies and television are accurate reflections of what masses of people accept as truth. If it pays, as it obviously does, to assert in dramatic charades week after week that "good" people are dull and "bad" people fascinating, it does so because this message strikes a responsive chord in all of us.

Now clearly there is no single inference to be drawn from the phenomenon of which I have been speaking. Other commentators, and I myself on other occasions, have pointed to various implications of this pattern in fiction. But one of the most important factors in the popularity of the antisocial hero, I am persuaded, is Western man's struggle to affirm his particularity, to define and defend his unique identity in the face of the universality of divine love and the selflessness implicit in the Christian ethic. There are two things which must be said in defense of that contention.

First, the appealing villains so common in modern fiction are in an important sense *life affirming* human beings. They attract us because, unlike the saint, they take this world with dreadful seriousness, such a great seriousness that they will not delay satisfactions. They act out in various ways, but always vividly, the determination to get what they want here and now. They would obviously rather have a crust today than pie-in-the-sky by-and-by.

Now it is important to notice that these mythical characters are not just ordinary thugs and degenerates. They are always given by their authors special qualities of personality. In any rogues' gallery they would stand out in significant ways. It is suggested, sometimes made explicit, that they do what they do for reasons more dramatic than those which motivate common criminals. The gangster collects antiques or breeds rare orchids. The safecracker is a connoisseur of diamonds. The western gunman loves the open spaces and finds humanity a blight upon the earth.

It is always suggested, you see, that these "bad" guys are more fully alive, more robustly passionate, more aware of the options, more willing to fight for what they want than their law-abiding fellow men. They have not been drained by convention, inhibited by fear, nor made frigid by piety. And however reprehensible their particular deeds, their lives are vivid and full.

Obviously such fictional characters are grotesque distortions of reality, three-dimensional caricatures of what they are intended to represent. What they seek in life may be and often is *inhuman* in the final analysis. But in their strange and perverse ways, they seem to dignify and even give a certain grandeur to the image of man. And we love them, I suspect, because of their relentless determination to accept and enjoy existence.

The second thing that must be said about the popularity of the villain in the mythology of our time is that it symbolizes the conviction that a degree of estrangement from the mass is essential to the development of both a strong character and a vital personality.

Notice that the hero in the kinds of stories of which I have been speaking is, above all, a lonely man. He is alienated from society by his urgent, ungovernable appetites. And he is isolated from his fellow villains by the sensitivity which makes him so special. There is, the myth seems to say, a dimension to personality which love, compassion, fellowship, justice, cooperation, and all the other virtues counseled by Christian piety cannot engender on their own. The lonely man of blood and violence riding off into the sunset is obviously the possessor of qualities to which the huddled homesteaders cannot hope to aspire.

(These reflections of mine may be caused by the fact that I once spent two weeks stranded on the Dalmatian coast of Yugoslavia with nothing to read but *Atlas Shrugged* by Ayn Rand. But we must leave such speculations to the higher critics and press on.)

We are often told by psychologists these days that the personality of a child takes on form over-against the personalities of its parents, that it is only as a child begins to assert itself; begins to affirm its own hopes, fears, and pretensions in defiance of its earlier more acquiescent role, that it acquires shape as an identifiable human being. We are assured that the rebellion must be a real one. It cannot be set up by the parents. It cannot be stage managed by Mother, role-played by Father, and kept within prearranged boundaries so as to do no damage to the furniture. There must be real blood, sweat, and tears. And one of the worst tricks that a family can play upon its offspring is to sponsor, subsidize, and thus disarm their rebellion.

Now it is important here to remember that this kind of filial resistance to parental authority is not something necessitated by errors in the parents' feelings and opinions. Its function is not that of protecting the truth, of defending the young against the falsehood cherished by the old. The inevitable rebellion is its own purpose. And it is as necessary where family authority is sensitively wise as where it is brutally stupid. To be fully human is to be in significant respects *self*-assertive.

The same principle can be applied more broadly, I think, and remain valid. Adult human beings never outgrow the need to achieve identity over-against other human beings. All of us need the pulling and hauling, the cut and thrust of antagonisms and interpersonal tensions. For it is these which compel us to define for ourselves what is really worth fighting for, to clarify, in short, the boundaries of our personal domains.

It is obvious that no human being can live without love. Without fellowship, human community, survival would not be worth its cost. But love is by its very nature self-*giving,* not self-*defining.* True fellowship draws men into a kind of communion which not only tears down interpersonal barriers, but often blurs interpersonal boundaries. The saint is likely to be dull, because he will not defend those lines by which he could be made a unique and interesting personality.

No amount of love can give an individual the special sense of his own identity which grows out of conflict. It is when our rough edges rasp against the rough edges of others that we discover painfully, which is the best way to discover anything, the myriad complex indentations which compose what we may have feared to be the featureless surface of our egos. It is this process of discovery which constitutes the beginning of a profound self-confidence. One might paraphrase Descartes and say, I resist; therefore I am. Paradoxically the alienation which makes us deeply conscious of our uniqueness gives us the courage to love.

You see, if I am to live in close association with other human beings without the loss of my own identity; if I am to become involved in the hopes, fears, joys, and sorrows of others and retain a distinguishable destiny of my own, I must have some defense against certain excessive forms of interpersonal trespass. I must be able to draw lines in specific situations and repel all efforts to cross them. I must be willing and psychologically able to strike out with ruthless force in response to dangerous assaults upon my separate self.

Unless I am willing to do these things, unless I am able to draw lines and resist ultimate invasions, the only alternative left me in defense of my person is to avoid all real fellowship in the first place, to find security in total and permanent isolation, a kind of estrangement which permits no reconciliations, because it recognizes no hostilities.

I have in mind here nothing so crude as mere distance or threats of massive retaliation, but something akin to the cocktail party syndrome in which men achieve both company and separation by the simple expedient of concealing themselves behind their smiles. Standing cheek to jowl they greet one another cordially and exchange *first* names with every appearance of sharing. But all the while they are divided by primordial chasms, remembering other fields, planning more exotic conquests, and waiting for the hostess to make them start circulating again.

There is nothing like a good fight to break up a cocktail party. Not because a fight injects hostility into the circle of friendship, but because it threatens to inject genuine encounter into the realm of meaningless proximity.

Yes, the cocktail party is the place to learn the game. But it *is* played elsewhere, especially in the Christian church. There is nothing like Christian love to keep men at a distance. If you would love nobody very much, love everybody very much. Love each and all with such an abundance of unstinted, undiscriminating, undemanding, and generalized good will that no man can claim you for his own. Let your love be so unconfined that it has no form, so all-embracing that it cannot tell one personality from another, so complete that all of its objects blend into one beloved, faceless mass!

Robert Browning in "My Last Duchess" tells of a duke who killed his wife. We do not know whether it was by direct action or by some more subtle means. But the reason for the deed is quite clear: "She liked whate'er she looked, and her looks went everywhere. . . . O, Sir, she smiled, no doubt, whene'er I passed; but who passed without much the same smile?" *

This is why men dislike saints. They like whatever they look on, and their looks go everywhere, and they smile at all who pass with much the same smile. But they do not *really love* anybody, any specific body. Not with the kind of love that normal men can understand, a love as conditioned and particular as the modes of history within which it must be expressed. A love so conscious of personality that it inevitably selects and discriminates. A love so intimate and personal that it always walks the narrow line between alienation and self-destruction.

You see, men cannot really appreciate a love which is directed toward the *concept* of mankind. They love particular, sinful individuals. And what they love about these individuals is not their human essence, but the most eccentric, relative, and perishable attributes: a smile, a tone of voice, a way of walking, a fierce determination to be noticed in a crowd, a tendency to blow up in heavy traffic. These are the kinds of things to which human love attaches itself. What we cherish in the people around us is not what they have in common, but what each of them has in a special way.

Whatever else we may have to say about the popular culture's appealing villains, they have not let themselves be digested by the mass. They are men and women who have insisted upon enough moral elbow room to permit the growth of personality. One always suspects that hidden beneath the violence and self-assertion there is a capacity to love and be loved which most of us know we lack.

It is not the least of the blessings of the cross of Jesus Christ that

---

* Robert Browning, *The Complete Poetic and Dramatic Works of Robert Browning* (Boston: Houghton Mifflin Co., 1895), p. 252.

makes it possible for us to be ourselves and to love others. For it is only when a man knows that he can be forgiven those acts of interpersonal aggression by which his personality is defined and the spasms of defensive violence by which his uniqueness is preserved that he can really be a man and run the terrifying risk of loving other men.

11
the two faces of faith

Advent is surely the most unsuccessful fragment of the Christian year. Liturgically it is a time of anticipation. Actually it is a season of profound nostalgia. Its appointed readings speak of the highway that is to be made straight in the desert for our God. But the autumnal mood which carried us "over the river and through the woods to grandmother's house" is not easily shaken. And that straight highway has little chance against the gentle curves and deceptive distances of Memory Lane.

We begin to sing, "Come, Thou Long-expected Jesus." But it sounds strangely like "Jingle Bells," the way "Jingle Bells" used to sound when faith was easy, because we had seen Santa Claus at J. L. Hudson's. And even the big boy next door who wrote dirty words on the sidewalk and blasphemed the Easter Bunny put away his chalk and walked softly in December. With the best of intentions we try to work up a mood of expectation, but find ourselves wondering whether it really snowed every Christmas Eve when we were young. Lectionary and liturgy to the contrary notwithstanding, the prevailing mood of Advent is a kind of nostalgia, the memory of earlier expectations.

Indeed, when we do look to the future in such a season as this, it is likely to be more in dread than in hope. Recollection of past partings and separations gives intimations of partings yet to come. And all add up to an effective definition of our mortality. Arthur Godfrey once flew his own airplane out of the city of New York late at night. As he looked down at what is surely one of the world's most breathtaking scenes, that vast metropolis swimming in its own light, he turned to his copilot and said, "It makes me so damned mad to realize that someday that will all be there. But I won't be around to see it." All of us have had feelings of the same kind; the sudden, keen, angry awareness of the frailty of our tenure among all that we have come to love.

One of the titans of Christian thought, it may have been Augustine or Aquinas, said that nostalgia should be numbered among the mortal sins. There is justice in that proposal, I am sure. Because the recurring homesickness to which man is subject can mortgage the possibilities of the future to the emotional engagements of the past. Like the moralistic sundial our memories record the sunny hours and make a hobby of invidious comparisons. No shore ahead is ever as beautiful, in fact, as the recollection of one left unwillingly behind. No challenges are as stirring, no friends as loyal, no books as engrossing, no teachers as profound as those enshrined in the desire to be young again. Nostalgia *can* turn memory against us and make yesterday the warder of tomorrow.

This same emotion often becomes, does it not, the means by which we enslave others. As a young man just starting out on a life of his own, I remember how deeply I resented the efforts of my elders to lay claim upon my new freedom with nostalgic appeals, constant reminders of the wonderful days of my earlier subordination. What new husband does not seethe when his family or his bride's tries to call one or the other of them back from the wholly engrossing new passion, back to former loyalties and older loves, by poignant references to times past and things shared? Times and things before *that other one* came along to spoil it all. "Billy, do you remember the way we used to . . ." And Billy is asked to affirm with a smile or tear that those were the great days and these, poor substitutes at best. Nostalgia has its obvious dangers. Perhaps it should be numbered among the mortal sins.

But before we surrender it to Augustine or even Aquinas, we must take some account of the profound homesickness which is at the heart of the biblical faith. It appears, of course, most dramatically in the Old Testament whose theology is often hard to distinguish from nostalgia. God may choose to identify himself to Moses in the present tense as "I am who I am." But Israel obviously prefers him in retrospect: the God of our fathers, the God of Abraham, Isaac, and Jacob, the One who fed us in the wilderness and gave us victory over the Amorites. He may be the Eternal sitting above the heavens. But he is more often acknowledged as some timely intervention in the past. The worship of Israel has something of the quality of a gazetteer, so that one finds it hard to separate revelation from real estate.

Indeed, the God of the Old Testament often lends aid and comfort to this mood when he speaks to his people as he so often does in the retrospective mode. "When Israel was a child I loved him; and out of Egypt I called my son. . . . It was I who taught Ephraim to walk, I took them up in my arms; . . . I led them with cords of compassion, . . . I bent down to them and fed them (Hos. 11: 1-4)." ("Billy, do you remember how we used to go to Belle Isle every Sunday afternoon to feed the swans? And one time you leaned out too far and fell into the lagoon? And I had to wrap you in the car robe until your clothes dried? And we laughed all the way home and had ice cream sodas at Sanders?")

Like all who have loved and are in danger of losing what they love, the mighty One of Israel is not above tugging at heartstrings with remembrance of things past. He binds men to him with cords not only of compassion but of memory. At times his mercy seems to reflect less of some transcendent, redemptive purpose than a kind of divine nostalgia. "How can I give you up, O Ephraim! How can I hand you over, O Israel (Hos. 11:8)!"

Well, this is in one respect the glory of Israel, is it not? That its God is remembered. Not simply believed in as a working hypothesis. Not merely acknowledged in rational fashion. Not defiantly affirmed as one affirms an unpopular truth. But remembered in an almost sensuous way, much as one recalls the dramatic moments of his personal past. Bricks without straw and the keys to the car. The parting of the Red Sea and the day school closed because of the snow. Manna in the wilderness and a coke at Joe's Drive-In. Joshua at Jericho and Pearl Harbor. There is about many Jews the kind of aplomb which comes of having in one's own parlor the things which other men see only in museums.

I sat one evening with friends who had spent the day closing out the family homestead, a house that had been theirs for over two hundred years. They were still engaged in sorting the smaller relics of a distinguished ancestry. As they spoke casually of this noted statesman and that famous general, one of them saw that I was looking on with the amused embarrassment of one whose roots are as shallow as crabgrass. Feeling self-consciously that something was called for, he said, "Muehl, you mustn't think that we are impressed over-much by the fact that we have distinguished forebears. There isn't much that we can do about it, you know. It just happens to be true."

This is the fate of even the most sophisticated Jew, is it not? Those who disclaim all the theology of the Bible are, like Prometheus, chained to his rocks. Even those who are not "impressed over-much" by their history are its prisoners. For Israel, faith is not a thing to be affirmed or denied. It is a memory which those who share it can never escape. It is for this reason that the Jews have been so bitterly persecuted time and time again. What sets them apart and makes them a threat to every closed system cannot be refuted, recanted, or outlawed. There is nothing that anyone can do about it. It just happens to be true. In the dungeons of the Inquisition, the ghettos of Poland, the sealed boxcars, and the death camps themselves, they *remember,* even as they pour out their lives. And count Jerusalem above their chief joy.

But if this is the glory and chief joy of Israel, it is also its infirmity, is it not? Chronicle became canon. The line between the tenses blurred. The assertion that God *had* acted in this way or that became the proclamation that God always acts in this way or that. The awful conviction that the Lord had said a particular thing to a specific people at an appointed place became the smug assurance that God says *only* that particular thing to those specific people at that appointed place. The nation whose theme had been, "The earth is the Lord's and the fulness thereof," surrendered to that cry of despair, "How shall we sing the Lord's song in a foreign land (Ps. 24:1; 137:4)?"

It is easy to lament the rigidity of Israel's memory of God. It is not difficult to diagnose Israel's failures. Honest nostalgia flows forward as well as backward. ("Someday that will all be there, but I won't be around to see it.") Poignant memories of the past have value only when they lend emotional force to expectation. Love experienced gives depth to love anticipated. Friends lost bequeath blessings of patience to friends unmet. Personal suffering remembered becomes compassion for suffering to be encountered. Nostalgia turns poisonous only when it flows in one direction, when it stifles expectation and kills hope. This is what happened to the memory of Israel. The very vividness of its experience of God made the mighty One the prisoner of his own record.

Even one who accepts this analysis of the Chosen People's frustration must do so with deep misgivings, because it is hard to see how it could have been otherwise. Can any man look upon the face of God and live? Can one stand in the presence of God and ever again feel eagerness to be elsewhere? Is it, in short, really possible to have a vivid experience of the Eternal and go on taking past, present, and future seriously? I cannot help feeling that Israel's fate is the unavoidable consequence of its glory. Its greatest sacrifice was the surrender of its authentic expectation. Having been made custodian of so vivid a memory of God, it became in the nature of things incapable of genuine hope. Its failure was inherent in its success. Its frustration the inevitable by-product of its obedience. Israel goes on speaking of the messianic promise. But the words have a liturgical ring to them and the voice lacks conviction. The Jews are the people who *remember* God.

In the presence of Israel's profound nostalgia, Christians are apt to feel an acute embarrassment. We are readers of the Book, but these people wrote it. We are bound to their faith by a few letters, an editorial postscript to the memoirs of Yahweh. We have been told that God can raise up children unto Abraham from the stones on the ground, but suspect that this was a hasty remark made in the heat of a family quarrel and are thus reluctant to count upon it. We are heirs of the promise. Yes, but heirs by adoption. And what heir old enough to remember the circumstances of his adoption ever overcomes completely the sense of estrangement? Even the youngest sibling, related to his brothers by blood, often feels uneasy in the presence of talk about things that happened before he was born and demands assurances that he was there, too; even if only "inside Mother."

How much more keenly is this insecurity felt by the adopted heir for whom the navel is not the symbol of a tie, but the ugly scar left where a tie was broken. The embarrassment which Christians feel in the presence of Israel's memory all too often turns into what might be called the *nostalgia of adoption,* the recollections which do not root in the experiences of one's own life but which grasp at the past of another. It is a remembrance which is conjured up or dearly bought to fill a vacuum in the heart. The colonial Briton is more English than the queen. The provincial Frenchman remembers Paris as only one who has never seen Paris could possibly remember it. The dependent relative who does not really belong in the family circle gathers and treasures the anecdotes of family life and repeats them in exhausting detail on all remotely appropriate occasions.

There is a neurotic intensity to secondhand memories; for they root not in what one has shared in the past, but in what one hopes desperately to be allowed to share in the future. So they lack the chastening and earthy realism of honest history and turn more quickly than most memory into dogma. "Oh, Billy never eats liver. . . . Oh, Billy will always have a second piece of chocolate cake." And this is said with such urgent and hopeful confidence that to take a bite of liver or refuse a piece of cake becomes an act of alienation.

The nostalgia of adoption has always been a threat to Christian faith. Never more so than in our own age. For most of us in the twentieth century are doubly disinherited, the victims of several estrangements. We do not remember Jerusalem. But neither do we remember Bethlehem, Rome, Avignon, Worms, Geneva, Canterbury, or for that matter the little brown church in the dell. Most modern men have no firsthand memory of God at all. We are not natural heirs of the shepherds for whom the skies opened and the angels sang. We are more the children of Twelfth Night, sons of the Magi who saw a star in the West and wondered what it might mean. Like our illustrious forebears we have had long journeys and stopped to ask directions in all the wrong places. And we feel alienated not only from Israel's memory of God but from the confident orthodoxies and self-authenticating traditions of our very brothers in Christ.

How doubly attractive, then, is the home that we have never really known. How tempting the ancient symbol, the bit of mysterious liturgy, the scrap of obliquely relevant dogma, and the esoteric vocabulary. How readily do we turn faith in upon itself in the search for ancestry, buying up old estates at auction, digging through dusty albums for striking resemblances, fabricating out of need and nothing a coat of arms that fools no one but ourselves. The nostalgia of adoption threatens in our time to turn the Christian faith into a sophisticated form of ancestor worship, all the more desperately retrospective because of its fear of being unmasked.

This spirit is understandable, of course. No man is an island and the need to know something of the terrain in which our personal experience of God occurred cannot be denied. But the effort, whatever its motive, to try to understand the Christian faith in retrospective terms is doomed to failure. Christians are not made orphans by the neglect of God. We are summoned to be orphans by the love of God. As Israel gave up its expectation in order to bear testimony to the historical reality of the divine, we are those who have been created without memory that we might live in expectation and witness with our lives to the continuing fulfillment of the promises made unto Abraham and his seed forever.

Israel's hope is the by-product of its memory and no stronger than that memory will permit it to be. Christian memory is the by-product of expectation and no more compelling than expectation can make it. We do not believe that Jesus Christ sits at the right hand of power because we remember that he rose from the dead. We remember that he rose from the dead, because we expect to find him daily at the right hand of power. Christians do not accept the claims of faith because the weight of accumulated evidence makes disbelief impossible. We expect the release of captives, the restoration of sight to the blind, and the liberation of the oppressed. And expecting these things, the fulfillment of ancient promises, we bear with some patience the claims of ancient creeds.

The thrust of the only persuasive Christian apology is forward. To seek the validation of the gospel in retrospective terms is an exercise in futility. As Israel is the prisoner of its memory, the Christian is the prisoner of hope. If you and I are able to proclaim with passion what God is alleged to have done in Christ, it is only because we await with confidence what Christ will do in us. In this lies the psychological component of the distinction between law and grace. Law reflects, grace expects. Law binds to the past. Grace commits to the future.

Thus, the Christian is always plagued by a sense of estrangement. This is his special calling. To be one who, not really belonging to the household of inherited certainties, can speak with compassion to a world which distrusts inherited certainties. To be one who, not remembering Jerusalem, seeks Christ in Scarsdale, Birmingham, Los Angeles, Detroit, and wherever the crowded ways of life converge. To be one who, always on the way to faith and never finally and irrevocably there, can best minister to a world that has been stripped of its faith, robbed of its hope, and left naked by the side of the road. To be one who, having no immediate antecedents of his own, feels most keenly his kinship with all men. To be one who, believing that the glory of the Lord is *to be* revealed, is determined that all flesh *shall* see it together.

Advent is inevitably one of the failures of the Christian year; for in the strange chemistry of our faith, recollection is a by-product of hope. The more passionately one expects, the more poignantly he remembers. The vision of what is to be gives deeper meaning to what has been. And to look forward with confidence is to look backward with gratitude.

12

the christian conspiracy against man

Several years ago at a party I was approached by a friend who had drunk more than he could handle. He stood swaying before me, glass in hand, and posed a truculent question. "Muehl," he asked, "if I believed all that Christianity bunk, do you know what I'd do?"

When I confessed that I could not possibly guess the direction of his purely hypothetical piety, he proceeded to enlighten me. "As soon as my children were born," he said, "I'd have them baptized. And then I'd cut their throats from ear to ear so they'd go straight to heaven. Now you tell me, if you can, why should any man who loves his kids let them go through the heartache of life and run the risk of hell, if he can send them to glory with a single sweep of the knife?"

Fortunately for me our hostess noted at this point that we had exchanged more than the dozen words appropriate to such occasions and interrupted to break up what she called our "little conference." My friend wandered back toward the bar, presumably to discover how many angels can dance on the top of a bottle, and I was led away to meet three "perfectly delightful" Vietnamese, who among them spoke somewhat less English than a cocker spaniel.

But that challenge troubled me long after the evening had ended. And it still does. Because, you see, it reflects the conviction that history can have no profound significance for the Christian, that the exclusive concern of the faith is the speedy liberation of man from "the heartaches and the thousand natural shocks" of the flesh. My intoxicated friend believed, and probably still believes for all the good that I was to him, that God is engaged only in the business of redemption. For him acceptance of Christian doctrine means rejection of the dignity of human existence.

One need not be drunk to make such a charge. Some of the greatest minds in the history of the church have worried about the same problem. Clement of Alexandria feared that the emphasis of piety upon an atoning *death* might rob life of its meaning. The philosopher-theologian Origen repeatedly tried to bridge what he regarded as the dangerous gap between the vitalities of history and the passivities of faith. And in our own time the Jesuit scholar Teilhard de Chardin charged that the greatest objection to Christianity is the fear that it dehumanizes people. Such concerns are easy to understand when one recalls that so eloquent a spokesman for a relevant piety as Ernst Troeltsch counted it one of the glories of the Christian gospel that God's mercy destroys the significance of all earthly distinctions.

Now the tragedy of this view of the cross, the notion that the action of which it is the center is the only ultimately significant action in history, that life can be fully realized and God known only in the events on Calvary, is that in its eagerness to exalt the truth made manifest in Jesus Christ it succeeds more often than not in debasing that divine self-disclosure. By trying to pour all that must be said of God into the symbolism of redemption, Christian piety tends to deprive that symbolism of its real meaning.

Let me try to explain what I mean here. The content of the New Testament is the proclamation of God's mercy. The Gospels and epistles are almost exclusively concerned with the revelation of divine compassion. One can, of course, find scattered through their pages words which have a prudential ring to them. But the primary thrust of the New Testament is redemptive in the most radical terms. In order to say what it means to convey, that the God who creates and judges also redeems, the gospel message undoubtedly subordinates both creativity and judgment to the most dramatic assurances of divine forgiveness. The words and deeds attributed to Jesus of Nazareth are almost invariably self-giving in a dramatic sense. Only occasionally does the Christ reveal any interest in justice as distinguished from charity. And he often rebukes those who urge upon him the burden of making careful distinctions or compromises. When he does speak of judgment, it is usually a technique, a means of throwing into more vivid contrast the compassion with which he is primarily concerned, much as an interior decorator uses accent points to enhance and emphasize his major color scheme.

As a result of this the effort to build a viable world view, a responsible ethical structure upon the basis of the New Testament is almost invariably an exercise in futility, a game for theologians which has no meaning for those who are not paid to play it.

This unhappy truth can be seen most clearly, of course, in that popular outgrowth of liberal theology, the emulation of the Jesus of the Gospels. For millions of modern Christians the ethical implications of the faith are quite clear. One is supposed to live as Jesus lived, dealing with people and events as he is reported in the New Testament to have done. The logic of this position is not hard to follow. If Jesus of Nazareth was the fullness of God enshrined in mortal flesh, if he was God's image of perfect manhood, then what Jesus said and did must outline clearly for the believer God's definition of the good life.

This imitation of the biblical Jesus has undoubtedly inspired some of history's most sacrificial devotion to the service of God and man. But it has also produced monumental hypocrisy, heartbreaking frustration, and the vulgarization of piety.

As an illustration of the first of these, monumental hypocrisy, one need only look to the businessman who professes to conduct his affairs as Jesus would have done. Or the politician who claims to govern by the principles of the Sermon on the Mount. One could not possibly run any business or govern any state successfully for five minutes in strictly New Testament terms. Those discriminating judgments, those prudential decisions, those just distinctions which are essential to all forms of human organization and survival are in radical conflict with the personal conduct and essential message of the Christ of the Gospels. The Jesus who exhorted his followers to walk the second mile, turn the other cheek, take no thought for the morrow, and give all that they have to the poor would have been an unmitigated disaster in any responsible position in the normal human community.

It is not strange that the Gospels portray the Christ as a wandering teacher, a man with little or nothing in the way of continuing obligations, one who could brush aside the entreaties of his family and even deny their special claim upon him. That is the only way in which he could have lived and faithfully fulfilled his divine commission. If he had settled down and accepted the burdens of sustained responsibility, his message would have been either badly blurred or radically changed.

It is no slander against the biblical Jesus to speak in such terms. By its very nature compassion is always to some degree irresponsible. That which takes account of justice, merit, social convenience, survival, value is not really mercy. At its best it is but a policy which counterfeits mercy for strategic purposes. And as such it may be both useful and praiseworthy.

But the redemptive love of God of which the New Testament

speaks is single-mindedly aimed at reclaiming the lost, healing the sick, and freeing the oppressed. It refuses to be inhibited by either prudence or necessity in its zeal to do these mighty works. And the medium by which this gospel is proclaimed, the form in which the message was made manifest is a life which can and does lend itself completely and freely to the substance of such a teaching. If Jesus of Nazareth had been the kind of man to whom one could look for advice in running a business or governing a state, he would by very definition have been incapable of embodying the mercy of God. To recognize this is no slur upon either Jesus or the responsible uses of power.

Thus, businessmen, politicians, and all others who allege that they conduct themselves daily as Jesus would have conducted himself in the same situations are either fools or liars. Jesus would have bankrupted any enterprise in five minutes and taken only slightly longer to turn the most orderly community into blood-soaked anarchy. The emulation of the Jesus of the Gospels is an utter impossibility and the theologian who offers it as a religious model makes hypocrites of his own disciples and a mockery of his vocation.

If hypocrisy and its attendant sins are the most obvious products of the Jesus cult, the heartbreaking frustrations which so often spring from the same source are surely more tragic in human terms. The world is littered with the ruins of Christian commitment and serious purpose which came to grief upon the futility of the Jesus ethic. When men *try* conscientiously to live in response to this radical expression of divine compassion, they inevitably find themselves assailed on the one hand by a sense of obvious irrelevance to the work of the world and on the other by a searing consciousness of their repeated failures to live up to the standard set for them by the Gospels.

First, they see power drift into the hands of more "practical" men, men who are more willing and able to take account of the need for justice in human affairs, men for whom judging, dividing, and taking thought for the morrow are a kind of second nature. Their own total dedication to the ethic of redemption again and again rules the imitators of the biblical Jesus out of any significant part in the moral dialogue going on around them. Once a man has made clear to his fellows his dedication to radical self-denial as a way of life, those who are engaged in the delicate business of trying to find viable paths through the relativities of history have little patience with his counsel. The views of the pacifist on foreign policy, for example, are seldom taken seriously, even by those who profess the highest regard for the pacifist's personal purity.

Now when one adds to this sense of irrelevance the inner awareness of just how far he has fallen short of his own high standards, the imitation of the New Testament Jesus becomes even more difficult to sustain. To be cut off from a significant role in the decision making of one's community might be a small price to pay for the achievement of moral perfection. But it becomes intolerably costly when one finds himself inevitably relaxing into attitudes and deeds which betray his own professions. One former New Testament absolutist put it in these words: "I used to find myself arguing eloquently for unselfish love as the only Christian way of life, while I coveted my host's library and lusted after his daughter."

No responsible ethic encourages either covetousness or lust. But there are many which take more realistic account of both than the cult of the New Testament Jesus.

Now I must pause here for a moment to note that some Christian ethicists have tried to bring the ethics of the New Testament to grips with reality by suggesting that the self-denying character of the life of Jesus is in fact the image of perfect manhood. But so perfect that it can only be admired and never really achieved by ordinary mortals.

Reinhold Niebuhr, for example, argues that the New Testament picture of Jesus is useful as an "unattainable ideal." To have the vision of this perfect man before us, he suggests, will be a perpetual guide and inspiration, even though in the very nature of things we cannot hope to reach anything approximating his perfection.

There is, of course, a significant measure of truth in this proposition. Humanity is always edified by its ideals and stirred to conduct consistent with them on many occasions. But there is one serious weakness in Niebuhr's reasoning. It overlooks the problem of frustration. A carrot held just beyond a donkey's nose will often motivate the beast to forward movement. But a carrot held so far beyond his nose that there is obviously no chance whatever of his reaching it will soon strike even a jackass as poor inducement for effort! And when the beast learns that the carrot has been placed beyond his reach on principle, he will either lie down in the traces or lash out with his heels at the one responsible for so absurd an arrangement. Dr. Norman Maier's experiments with rats demonstrated clearly that too great a gap between ideal and possibility induces not increased effort but *literally* paralyzing frustration.

The fundamental defect in the attempt to build a way of life upon the basis of the New Testament revelation alone is, of course, the mistaken assumption that God's will for humanity *is* fully revealed in the personality of Jesus, that the Christ, whatever more he may be, is God's picture of the perfect man.

The obvious fact, which only misguided piety could obscure, is that the Jesus of the Gospels, far from being the essence of human perfection, is only the merest fragment of an authentic human personality. He is composed of brief glimpses, transient relationships, vaguely remembered speeches, and contradictory definitions. Taken together these do not add up to a full character. The best resources of biblical scholarship and theological imagination working in concert have been unable to give us more than a sketch upon which to base the inferences of piety. For the Gospel writers the Christ was the incarnation of divine mercy. And what they remembered and wrote about him reflects both the majesty and the limitations of that view. Their concern was not to outline some image of perfect man but to proclaim what they had seen enshrined in a particular man, the depth of God's compassion. The New Testament does not reveal what all men are to be. It discloses, rather, that divine forebearance which makes *being* itself possible.

And so, if we are honest, we must be prepared to admit that the effort to imitate Jesus and make an ethical system of his life leads to perfectionist irrelevance and personal frustration.

But there is one more thing to be said. And it is probably the most damaging blow to the cult of the New Testament Jesus. So let's put it briefly and then fill in the detail. The Jesus of the Gospels is not really an *appealing* ideal upon which to model human personality. The repeated efforts which have been made to represent him as everything from a robust Rotarian to a crusading, left-wing radical have been remarkably less than successful because of the severe shortage of usable material. Jesus obviously cared nothing for most of the central concerns of normal human beings. In his fanatic determination to proclaim the redemptive love of God, he clearly shut out of his life those very relationships and responsibilities which dignify and ennoble human existence. There is no evidence that he ever married, raised a family, earned a living, or involved himself in the social and political problems of his community. Nor have we any reason to suppose that he either valued or understood the richly diverse creativities of the pagan world around him. He saw himself as the bearer of one mighty commission. And in faithfulness to his task he impoverished himself, poured out his life, and narrowed his personality in radical fashion.

If all men were to model themselves upon the historical Jesus, the world would be in many respects a better place than it is now. But it would be in at least as many respects a poorer place than it is now. A mankind radically committed to mercy as the primary dynamic of life would leave undone those acts of creativity, would leave unborne those burdens of justice without which history would degenerate into a swamp of compassion.

I suspect that we have reached the point at which a good solid illustration is in order. Fortunately we have one at hand. I refer to the impact of the Jesus cult upon Christian attitudes toward sex. Jesus of Nazareth is represented in the Gospels as having led a celibate existence. He had no wife, and surely no mistress. As a result Christian theology has through the ages been deeply embarrassed in its approach to human sexuality. Looming like a dark cloud over every religious discussion of male-female relationships is the fact that this allegedly *perfect* man, this divine conception of ideal humanity, managed to achieve and sustain his supremely perfect existence without the benefit of any sex life whatever. The result has been a deeply planted, strongly rooted inability on the part of Christians to treat sex without shame. And the whole absurd charade reaches its incredible climax in those Roman Catholic Pre-Cana Conferences which hold up the holy family as the model of domestic bliss, while steadfastly proclaiming the perpetual virginity of Mary.

And what is so obviously, dramatically true in the field of sex is equally true, though less vividly, in economic, social, political, and cultural respects. The world is filled with pale and shallow lives which justify themselves in terms of a distorted image of New Testament morality. Because Jesus never went to college, never read a novel, never wrote a poem, because Jesus did not dance, kiss women, or run for public office, millions of well-meaning Christians feel morally queasy whenever they do any of these things. They are not quite sure how such Old Testament activities fit into the El Greco world that is supposed to have begun on Calvary.

Thus, there is a vulgarity about the religious life of Western man, a vulgarity which inevitably infects all other aspects of his existence. Because we know so much more about what Jesus did *not* do than about what he did, the Christian personality has been defined in largely negative terms. This definition has in turn stunted the creative energies of whole societies.

Why should any man let his children go through the heartaches of life and run the risk of hell? This is the kind of question which inevitably arises when the Christ event is lifted from its biblical context and made the central focus of theology. And there is no answer to it in strictly New Testament terms. For while the gospel tells us how man is saved, it does not tell us what man *is*. That is the function of the Old Testament. And the Old Testament's answer to the tipsy question can be stated in one sentence. A man lets his children go through the heartaches of life and run the risk of hell, because it is heartache and risk which create the only thing worth redeeming, an authentic human being.

13
man in free fall

In his provocative book *The Great Divorce* the English lay theologian, the late C. S. Lewis, told of an Anglican bishop who was so broad-minded that he refused to go to heaven, because he had heard that there is no freedom of discussion there.

Whatever the wisdom of this prelate's personal decision, his basic assumption is in all probability correct. Real freedom of discussion can exist only where there is some reasonable difference of opinion about the truth of a proposition. Where the validity of any thesis is beyond doubt, argument ceases to be a creative use of freedom and turns into either whimsy or corruption. If you have ever listened to one of those adolescent college debates on some such topic as, *Resolved: that men make better fathers than mothers;* if you have suffered through such an exercise in rhetorical futility, you are familiar with the triviality of debate about an obviously true statement. Real freedom of discussion assumes the ambiguity of truth. And there can be no ambiguity about truth in that state of perfect union with God which men call heaven.

Indeed, one might extend the bishop's principle and affirm that no freedom of any kind is possible without serious and persuasive differences in men's views of truth. To know *fully* the precise nature of ultimate reality would be to understand both the character of the good life and the means appropriate to its achievement. And such knowledge would destroy freedom more finally than the most vicious tyrant could ever hope to do. Historical freedom is based upon the inevitability of error in every human calculation.

This vexatious relationship between freedom and inevitable error is for me the real meaning of the story of the fall with which the biblical biography of man begins. All too often those of us who feel called upon to preach about that familiar myth ignore what I would contend is the most significant aspect of it, and argue wrongly that it is *choice itself* which constitutes the essential element in the historical freedom of the human race. And to say this, i.e., that the essence of freedom is merely the power to choose, is to overlook the two-part character of the fall and misunderstand at critical points the grandeur and tragedy of man's existence.

When Adam yielded to his wife's invitation and ate of the fruit of the Tree of the Knowledge of Good and Evil, both he and Eve were immediately transformed. Even before God discovered their crime, they became self-conscious about their nakedness and suffered a dramatic change in personality. The initial stage in their punishment appears to have been the loss of their former total compatability with their environment. The moment they learned to distinguish between good and evil they became creatures of choice and decision. From that point on their relationship to the world around them was one of critical responsibility, not instinctive harmony. Man ceased to be the confident beneficiary of creation and became instead both its conqueror and its victim. Having reached out for the power to judge, he was compelled to exercise that power. Judgment became an inherent part of life, an obligation as well as an ability. Man could no longer do what came naturally, but must in every area of his existence examine, analyze, select, discriminate, weigh, decide, and choose. Then in retrospect praise and blame.

Now if the consequences of Adam's first disobedience had ended at that point, humanity might have retained its ability to discover fully the will of God, to see the truth with unobscured vision. The process would admittedly have been far more complex than before the fall, requiring the exercise of various frail powers of discernment and will. But so long as Adam and Eve remained in Eden, that is, continued in the presence of the Eternal, the achievement of something very like their former harmony with the cosmos was not inherently impossible.

But then came the second part of their punishment. When God learned of the forbidden act, he drove the man and woman out of Eden and set the cherubim with the flaming sword at the gate to see that they never returned.

If the Garden of Eden is understood to be a state of compatability between the will of God and the mind of man, Adam's expulsion from the garden clearly represents for the biblical writer the final separation of man from even the possibility of a complete understanding of God's nature. The world into which Adam was driven and in which his descendants are still imprisoned by the flaming sword is *by definition* the realm of imperfect perception of the truth. From now on, the Bible says, man will never again look directly at God, but only at his distorted reflection in the dark mirrors of history.

This fact is made quite explicit in the book of Exodus. Moses is told by Yahweh that no man can look upon the face of the

Eternal and live. Now unless we decide to go anthropomorphic at this point and imagine God as an aging prima donna who threatens violence to anyone who sees her sans make-up, we are bound to interpret the passage in Exodus to mean that there is an inescapable contradiction between a fully *human* existence and an unobstructed vision of the divine. Life is defined biblically as the partial, fragmentary, and inadequate experience of God. Man is forbidden to look upon God not in order to protect the dignity of the Almighty, but in order to preserve his own humanity.

Well, this is what C. S. Lewis' bishop believed. That what makes man human is his determination to exercise the power to make significant choices, that his essential freedom is dependent upon his estrangement from God. This is not an easy doctrine to accept. It goes against the grain of much classical philosophy. And there are certainly biblical texts which can be adduced to contradict it. So insidious is its power that it has even split the ranks of a resurgent American conservatism, driving a wedge between such close partners as William Buckley and his brother-in-law Brent Bozell. Mr. Bozell holds that it is better to be virtuous than free, while Mr. Buckley has apparently never had to face the choice.

Human resistance to this disturbing implication of the fall is perfectly understandable. We all long to believe that the possibility of comprehending God is a live option, that someone somewhere has the magic word by which the scattered fragments of our vision of truth can be drawn together into a perfect and familiar portrait of the Eternal. This yearning for easy answers to ancient questions is no weaker for its antiquity. Nor is it the eccentric passion of philosophers and theologians. Obviously one need not be the victim of an excess of piety in order to understand how useful it could be to think God's thoughts one step ahead of him.

The urge is not always expressed in religious terms. The literature of the Western world abounds in treatises which purport to disclose the simple principle by which life can be coherently organized and all problems solved. They are the works of psychologists, sociologists, economists, politicians, and salesmen, as well as metaphysicians. And they range from weighty tomes in which there is much useful wisdom to slender pamphlets extolling the therapeutic values of abdominal breathing. Some of history's foremost men appear to have put great store by daily exercise, cold showers, and blackstrap molasses.

But when all the esoteric formulas have been tried, when the pieces of the puzzle have been arranged and rearranged in an infinite variety of ways, God remains the one who is visible, if at all, in snatches, visions, and dreams. And truth is best defined as the most viable error.

This obviously renders life a painful enterprise. What we do not know always hurts us in one way or another. We learn at an early age that the ambiguities which make freedom possible make suffering inevitable. One cannot be both free and secure within any profound definition of either term.

So men are forever tempted to limit their personal liability, to try to dispel some of the painful ambiguity which surrounds their lives by imposing significant limitations upon their own freedom. We offer God a sort of bargain: "If you, O mighty One of Israel, will be less than fully divine, we agree to be less than fully human. Let's go on playing this game called 'history.' But not for keeps. Or let's at least set a house limit so that no one loses too much. Give us some guidelines by which we can inhibit our passionate humanity and avoid the most terrifying implications of our finitude."

This is a pretty fair description of much that we call "morality," is it not? The effort to reduce the Almighty to manageable size by mutilating his image in man. If we can just make man small enough, if we can somehow stunt his fearful potentiality, we may be able to diminish the massive reality of God, much as one might try to control the speed of an automobile by twisting the speedometer dial on the dashboard. So we define the good life in negative terms, cast religious reflections upon creative energies, and make saints of pious nonentities whose chief claim to fame is their shortage of red corpuscles!

Sören Kierkegaard reacted to this undertaking and its consequences in a famous passage in his *Either/Or:*

> Let others complain that this age is wicked. My complaint is that it is paltry and lacks passion. Men's thoughts are thin and flimsy like lace, too trivial to be sinful. . . . It might be sinful for a worm to harbor such thoughts. But not for a being made in the image of God. . . . This is the reason my soul

always turns back to the Old Testament and to Shakespeare. Those who speak there are at least human beings. They love, they hate, they murder their enemies, and curse their descendants through all generations. They sin.*

These words are flesh on the bone of Martin Luther's famous exhortation to "sin boldly."

Now, of course, Kierkegaard and Luther were in a sense playing with the word "sin" in order to make a point. So am I. And *my* point is this: To be truly human is to be at war with every absolute, including God. For to be truly human is to take this world with what comes as close to an ultimate seriousness as man can achieve. It means seeing eternal implications in all of the relativities of history, a willingness to commit one's self to myriad fragments of the truth, to struggle, fight, and die at the behest of what are admittedly equivocal causes. To be truly human is to point to faint shadows cast upon clouds by fleeting moments and say of them, "Lo, here" or "Lo, there. . . ." "This is the will of God. . . . That is the hand of the Eternal. . . . Thus saith the Lord."

It is, you see, the universal, inescapable, paradoxical destiny of man to know that all good is a distorted reflection of the divine, to understand that what is best in life is a mere intimation of the absolute, and yet to love those relative goods and bend to their service every resource of heart, mind, and spirit. To remember that there was a place called "Eden" in which God was fully known, but not let moral nostalgia drain the vitality from life and the meaning from history.

Nowhere is this problem set forth more vividly than in that perplexing Old Testament book Ecclesiastes, the writing of the preacher *Koheleth*. For centuries scholars in both the Jewish and Christian communities have carried on a continuing debate about the nature of this work. Some say that the book was written by King Solomon over a long period of time, so that it represents the changing views of an aging man. Others argue that the work is actually a dialogue in which two authors carry on a debate about the nature of human existence. And a few commentators go so

---

* Sören Kierkegaard, *Either/Or*, tr. David F. Swenson and Lillian Marvin Swenson with revisions and a foreword by Howard A. Johnson, p. 22. Copyright 1944 © 1959 by Princeton University Press; Princeton Paperback, 1971. Used by permission.

far as to postulate three participants, two antagonists and a moderator or interlocutor.

What troubles scholars is that the book of Ecclesiastes is a strange mixture of piety and impiety, belief and disbelief, wide-eyed wonder and cynical, world-weariness, all strung together in a single literary structure.

Koheleth says in one moment, "A good name is better than precious ointment," but then he goes on, "and the day of death, than the day of birth." He advises, "Rejoice, O young man, in your youth, and let your heart cheer you in the days of your youth; walk in the ways of your heart and the sight of your eyes." But then he concludes, "But know that for all these things God will bring you into judgment. . . . Behold, all is vanity and a striving after wind." Again he writes, "Wisdom gives strength to the wise man more than ten rulers that are in a city," only to add a moment later, "The wise man has his eyes in his head, but the fool walks in darkness; and yet I perceived that one fate comes to all of them (Eccles. 7:1; 11:9; 1:14; 7:19; 2:14)."

In the book of Ecclesiastes, Koheleth expounds poetically the essentially paradoxical character of life in history. Man, says the preacher, cannot rise above himself far enough or long enough to make objective judgments about the overall meaning of his existence. What he can know about the purposing will of God is sharply limited by the relationship between the whole and its parts. ("He has put eternity into man's mind, yet so that he cannot find out what God has done from the beginning to the end [Eccles. 3:10].") Man will always be driven in opposed directions and torn by conflicting desires, because both direction and desire are by-products of his finiteness. ("For that is his lot [Eccles 3:22].") God has given his creature just enough transcendence, says Koheleth, to enable him to see something of the majesty of his existence but not enough to let him comprehend the larger design of which his life is a tortured part. ("Then I saw all the work of God, that man cannot find out the work that is done under the sun. However much man may toil in seeking, he will not find it out; even though a wise man claims to know, he cannot find it out [Eccles. 8:16].")

Koheleth sees life as a series of inevitably inadequate responses to inherently limited conceptions of the Eternal. In his efforts to fulfill the divine will, he says, man is bound to fail. But the inevitability of failure cannot be made the excuse for refusing to act. Any retreat from the complexity of God, especially retreat into nonbeing or partial-being, is the most terrible depravity. Piety is for the author of Ecclesiastes that faith in the ultimate meaning of existence which enables man to accept his paradoxical destiny without despair. And sin is the effort to retire from life into bland neutrality or make something less than the whole will of God the ordering principle of survival.

> For everything there is a season and a time for every matter under heaven:
> a time to be born, and a time to die;
> a time to plant, and a time to pluck up what is planted;
> a time to kill, and a time to heal; . . .
> a time to weep, and a time to laugh; . . .
> a time to love, and a time to hate;
> a time for war, and a time for peace.
> —Ecclesiastes 3:1-4, 8

> In the morning sow your seed, and at evening withhold not your hand; for you do not know which will prosper, this or that, or whether both alike will be good.
> —Ecclesiastes 11:6

Even though it is inevitable, says Koheleth, that man's best will be shattered against the awful perfection of God and that his finite vision will set him against himself and his fellows, this inevitability cannot be made the excuse for withholding his hand. The first purpose of life is living. No man may say, if I do not plant, I shall not have to reap; if I do not wound, I shall not have to heal; if I do not love, I shall not have to hate. For to say these things is to mean, if I do not really live, I may never have to die.

The eternal God stands over against all of the sights, sounds, and textures of existence which we define as life in freedom. And to be human is to be at war with God, because it is to affirm historical realities which fall far short of perfection and yet lay claim upon our devotion in ultimate ways. The awful fact about original sin is not that it is an attribute of human personality, some uncontrollable impulse resident in every man, but that it is the essence of *truly human* personality. Its strength lies not in its power to corrupt the will, but in the fact that it is the taproot of all that flowers majestically from the tree of human freedom.

There is not an honest man on earth who longs to return to Eden, who would willingly "cancel and tear to pieces that great bond which keeps us pale." For to return to Eden would be to sacrifice all that makes us men. And no truly human being can yearn for such a fate, no matter how appealing it may seem to angels.

This, then, is why the cross of Jesus Christ is so essential to our hope. Because we cannot go back to Eden, *will* not go back to Eden, God comes out to us. Because the absolute, the infinite, the eternal cannot be confronted in history without destroying history, God becomes less than the absolute, the infinite, the eternal. He submits himself to the processes by which our humanity is defined. He accepts the conditions of our mortality and subjects himself to the suffering and dissolution which they make inevitable. And in so doing he consecrates history for all ages to come. Not by transforming it into something other than history. But by consenting to know and be known within the bloody and turbulent relativities of man's daily life. On Calvary God surrendered and recognized the state of rebellion as the realm of our proper human fulfillment.

Those who take their lives seriously are still at war with every absolute, including God. But now it is a war without hatred, a conflict without guilt. Truth is still perceived only in fragments. But those fragments are understood to be nothing less than the broken body of Christ.

epilogue

From time to time I have a nightmare in which I find myself in hell. It is not a very interesting place and owes more to Dante than to Sartre. In it the damned are buried up to their necks in the traditional Lake of Fire, their condition apparently hopeless. But around the edges of the lake moves a compassionate angel who is determined to save as many of its victims as possible. From time to time he manages to reach out and grip the hand of one of the tormented souls and tries with all his angelic strength to pull it from the flames. For a moment it appears that the effort will succeed, and a fragrance of something like hope can be detected in the smoke. But at the last second the angel slips, falls, and lets the sufferer sink back into the fire. As the flames mount up to claim their victim once more, a chorus of demons on the opposite bank cries out, "Now don't be angry with the angel, friend. He's doing his best."

In some respects modern Christians are like the hell-bound angel in my dream. The prophetic zeal of their pulpits has made them keenly aware of human suffering. More of them than cynics will admit reach out their hands in one way or another in the service of redemptive love. They are eager to "save" people from the torment of social, economic, political, and psychological despair. But their efforts are doomed at the outset by a definition of faith which makes it little more than a synonym for sincerity. The beneficiaries of their compassion are the victims of their simple-mindedness, and the initiatives of hope are doomed by ignorance to intensify human pain.

Both God and life are complex: the primary dimension of each is infinite mystery. In consequence man might almost be defined as the *anxious* creature. To suggest that good intention has no place in Christian doctrine would be wrong, but to make it the major part of piety is a disaster. The mind is at least as important an instrument of grace as the heart, and understanding the facts contributes as much to the redemption of the world as willing the good. If anything is more blasphemous than the suggestion that the Christian life is easy, it is the promise that it can be kept simple.